Anne Ridge

DEATH CUSTOMS IN RURAL IRELAND
Traditional Funerary Rites in the Irish Midlands

ARLEN
HOUSE

Published in 2009 by
ARLEN HOUSE
an imprint of Arlen Publications Ltd
PO Box 222
Galway
Ireland
Phone/Fax: 00 353 86 8207617
Email: arlenhouse@gmail.com

Distributed in North America by
SYRACUSE UNIVERSITY PRESS
621 Skytop Road, Suite 110
Syracuse, NY 13244–5290
Phone: 315–443–5534/Fax: 315–443–5545
Email: supress@syr.edu

ISBN 978–1–903631–76–8, *paperback*

An Chomhairle Oidhreachta
The Heritage Council

This publication has received support from the Heritage
Council under the 2008 Publications Grant Scheme

Typesetting ¦ Arlen House
Printing ¦ Betaprint

CONTENTS

ACKNOWLEDGEMENTS

I wish to thank most sincerely Dr. Pádraig Ó Héalaí, for his interest in my research, for sharing his knowledge and for his guidance.

I wish to acknowledge the assistance of Clodagh Doyle of the Museum of Country Life, National Museum of Ireland, Turlough Park, County Mayo, in helping to source photographs of John Connaughton, William Egan, and Patrick Johnson and John Kenny. I am very grateful to Finbarr Connolly, Rights and Reproduction Office, National Museum of Ireland, Collins Barracks, Dublin, for his courtesy and assistance in providing me with the photographs.

My thanks are due to the Allen family of Williamstown, Mount Temple, Co. Westmeath, for facilitating my visit to Mrs Annie Allen. Special thanks to Marie Allen for taking me along the Pilgrims' Road, Clonmacnoise, and arranging for me to meet Gertie Johnson, daughter of Patrick.

I am very grateful to Larry Gallagher, James Hanley and Tony Dooner, of Longford Sub Aqua Club, for taking me to Inchcleraun and Inchbofin on Lough Ree. Thank you to the members of W.A.H. Soc. who have accompanied me on trips to graveyards, especially Jo, Mary and Maisie.

I wish to thank the following people for permitting me to use their photographs: Edward Egan for the photograph of Kieran Mc Manus and the funeral photograph given to him by Mrs B. Egan Mitchell, Rosaleen Fallon for photograph of cot funeral, William Gacquin for the use of the photograph of Knockcroghery, given him by Mrs. Honoria Butler, Nuala Nevin for the photograph of her grandfather Tommy Lucas, and to Christy Cunniffe for sourcing it for me, John Murray for the photograph of his mother Anne Murray, John O'Connor for photographs from Killinvoy and Kilronan graveyards, Noel O'Neill for photograph of the Joyce monument and Liam Taylor for the photograph of Tom Kelly. I would like also to thank Albert Siggins for his drawing of the crossed shovels and spades and Jim Ganly for deciphering the Murry headstone for me.

Special thanks to Tom Harney for introducing me to Edward Egan, Drum, County Roscommon and Tom Kelly, Curraghboy, County Roscommon. My thanks are due also to James Dockery, Marian Harlow, Vincent Harney, Gerry

O'Brien, Mary O'Connell, Nollaig Mc Keon, Thomas Shaughnessy and Albert Siggins. I wish to acknowledge the assistance of Breeda Gilligan and Cáit Browne of Roscommon County Library, Mary Dillon of Ballinasloe Library, and the staff of the James Hardiman Library at NUI Galway and Galway County Library.

Special thanks are due to Alan Hayes of Arlen House for his professional support.

Finally, I would like to acknowledge the support of my family, Paul, Enda, Mary and my sister Mary.

LIST OF ILLUSTRATIONS

Death as an important rite of passage has been documented in an extensive body of literature and folklore internationally.

> The study of death rituals is a positive endeavour because, regardless of whether custom calls for festive or restrained behaviour, the issue of death throws into relief the most important cultural values by which people live their lives and evaluate their experiences. Life becomes transparent against the background of death, and fundamental social and cultural issues are revealed.[1]

The present text discusses burial customs in a part of Ireland that has not received any substantial attention to date in published literature, namely the midlands with a particular focus on County Roscommon. The evidence relates also to adjoining parts of counties Galway, Mayo, Sligo, Leitrim, Longford, Westmeath and Offaly.

Folklore is recognised as a valuable source for the study of ideas and observances concerning death. The present study is based in part on folklore collected in the late 1930s and especially on that recorded by James Delaney, a full time collector with the Irish Folklore Commission in the 1950s, 60s and 70s. 'That body (The Irish Folklore Commission) was responsible for the collection, preservation, classification, study and exposition of all aspects of Irish folk traditions until 1971, when it was replaced by the Department of Irish Folklore and incorporated into University College Dublin'.[2] The majority of informants recorded by Delaney were aged 65 to 90 years and they recounted customs which they had experienced in their youth or which they had heard of from an earlier generation. Their evidence therefore relates directly to the last half of the nineteenth century and the first decades of the twentieth century and also embodies older material.

Folklore recorded in a particular country often has parallels in other traditional societies. Death has been the subject of investigation in well-known international studies notably: van Gennep's *Rites of Passage*, Frazer's *Fear of the Dead in Primitive Religion*, Ariès's *The Hour of*

Our Death, and Christansen's *The Dead and the Living.* Other material drawn on includes articles in *Folklore: A Quarterly Review of Myth, Tradition, Institution, and Custom,* the Journal of the British Folklore Society and *Béaloideas: Iris an Cumann le Béaloideas Éireann.* These sources are referred to as pertinent in order to contextualise the material for the midlands. The study is divided into three chapters which deal with the customs associated with death, the wake, removal and burial. For each stage of death, wake, removal and burial the various rituals are discussed in a temporal sequence.

Notes

[1] P. Metcalf, R. Huntington, *Celebrations of Death: The Anthropology of Mortuary Ritual,* New York 1991, 25.

[2] B. Almqvist, 'The Irish Folklore Commission Achievement and Legacy', *Béaloideas* 45 (1977), 6-26; 9.

Chapter One

DEATH

In all cultures, established customs were observed at the time of death and similarities may be discerned in the traditions between Ireland and the wider European area in particular. Rituals practised at the time of death were important for a variety of reasons and were based on both Christian and Pagan beliefs. In Irish tradition, many of the same customs existed in every county. Thus, there are similarities in the funerary traditions in the midland counties but variations exist also, between counties and even between townlands within counties. It is generally recognised that traditional customs practised at the time of death helped the dying and the survivors to cope with the event, both spiritually and physically. Although people accepted death they also feared it; thus, the dangers associated with the event were controlled by ritual which protected the living and the dying. A number of distinct rituals may be identified associated with omens, rites of passage, the preparation of the corpse, laying out of the corpse, the use of holy water and candles.

Death Omens
Death is a central and inevitable part of the human condition and its importance is manifested in belief in omens associated with the event. In mythology, death was preordained and significant:

> It is noteworthy that folk/belief is in agreement with the myths. However 'sudden' the death, there will have been omens. An apple/tree will have blossomed out of season, a hen will have crowed like a cock, or a dog will have howled at night. Someone will have seen a corpse/candle or a phantom/funeral or there will have been a premonitory dream or an inexplicable uneasiness.[1]

In folk tradition throughout Europe different signs announced death and some of these are referred to by historian, Steven Wilson, in *The Magical Universe*:

> Very common was the howling of a dog, especially at an unusual time, or the cry or just the appearance of a bird. Tapping on windows by magpies or robins was also noted as an omen of death in England and Ireland.[2]

Similar signs were observed in the Ballymoe area on the border between counties Roscommon and Galway:

> A sure sign was when four of five dogs answer each other in a crying bark; if a cock came in front of a door and crows, also a hen crowing or a wisp dangling from the tail of a hen; a willie wag-tail hopping near the kitchen door; a magpie hopping in the street opposite the dwelling house.[3]

According to Bardan (author of *The Dead Watchers and Other Folk-Lore Tales of Westmeath*), the howling of a dog near the house of a sick person as an omen of death 'is ascribed on scientific grounds to the animal's keen sense of the odour of approaching dissolution'.[4] In south Roscommon, it was recorded that:

> A wisp of straw in a hen's tail is the sign of a death. If a grave sinks soon after burial it is the sign of another death in that family soon. The grave must sink soon after the burial.[5]

Among other signs of death recorded in the Boyle area in north Roscommon in the late 1930s were:

> The cock crowing twelve times before the usual hours of twelve and four; an uneven number of swans passing over a house; a waste spot appearing in a crop; a black hare approaching a house; five magpies approaching a house together; dreaming of marriage or straw or that you saw a grave opened; a curl on a lake on a calm day was a sign of a drowning; if a person fell in a fort or a graveyard; if a frog came into a house; if two sets of gloves or an extra cap were put in by mistake when a habit was bought, another death would follow.[6]

Similar customs were collected over thirty years later in northwest Offaly from narrator William Egan who also believed that dreams were significant.[7] There were many superstitions concerning birds and in the folklore material investigated they were usually seen as a bad omen. Birds were not to be trusted as if some malign spirit were associated with them, according to Lady

Wilde (author of *Ancient Cures, Charms and Usages of Ireland*). 'They come and go, according to popular belief, with significant messages from the unseen world of good or bad omen, but generally with warnings and prophecies of doom'.[8] People were superstitious about crickets as it was felt that the cricket could foretell death: 'If there is a death about to take place in a house, the cricket will sing louder than usual for a month before the event'.[9]

Throughout the country, it was believed that the cry of the banshee (the Irish supernatural death-messenger) predicted death. Belief in the banshee has been widely recorded in folklore and her existence can be traced back to the eighth century. Patricia Lysaght of the Department of Folklore at University College Dublin cites the *Táin Bó Fraích* [The Cattle Raid of Froech] which is set in the court of Mebh and Ailill at Cruachain in Roscommon in which Froech (son of Mebh) is wounded and is brought to the fort of Cruachain. (Medb, mythological queen of Cruachain and her husband Ailill, resided at Cruachain) While his wounds are being attended to there, the sound of weeping is heard over Cruachain and one hundred and fifty beautiful women are seen. Froech hears their lamenting and says, 'This is the crying of my mother and of the women of Boand' [*Gol mo mátharsa inso agus bantrochta Bóinni*].

> One can discern a relationship between the weeping women in this text and the death-messenger of the archival records. First of all, the lamenting women are *mná side* (plural of *ben síde*) and they are crying for Froech who is to die – they carry him into the subterranean abode of the dead, *Síd Crúachan*. It seems therefore, that *ben side* in the meaning 'supernatural death-messenger' can be dated to the eighth century.[10]

The banshee was heard but rarely seen and it was felt that she was not of this world. Lysaght says '*táim féin sásta gur fhéach na daoine uirthi mar neach ar leith ó na síoga*' ['I'm satisfied that people looked upon her as being distinct from the fairies'].[11] In the Shannon region of northwest Offaly:

> Sometimes the banshee is heard a week or a fortnight before anyone is to die. Other times she cries the night or so before. She is supposed to be a woman with yellow hair and she generally do be seen combin' her hair and cryin'.[12]

In practically all accounts from the midlands, she was heard at nightime but James Grady of St John's Parish, Athlone, described hearing her in the morning on his way to school:

> The cry was coming from the same spot, and there was a forge above near the school and there was a whole lot of men there waiting to get jobs done, and all ran out in the street to listen and no one seen her. She always cried after two families in this locality, the Grady's and the Diffley's. There did two children - two gossoons - die the same day with scarlet fever. They were belonging to Pat Grady and they were second cousins of my own.[13]

The keening of children by the banshee is not a widely recorded tradition. As reported by Lysaght the banshee was:

> Only very rarely thought to follow children. These, especially infants, were not regarded as full members of the family. The infant mortality rate of former times might have meant that too much notice would not normally be paid to the death of a young child.[14]

In the Parish of Columcille, Longford it was recorded that:

> The banshee cries for certain families, the Flynns, Floods, Farrellys and the Kanes, or any family beginning with an "O". They say the banshee is the spirit of the keeners that used to cry for the old Irish families.[15]

In Moor, south Roscommon, the narrator heard the banshee before her uncle died:

> My father's people were Burkes and the banshee always cries when anyone of the family is goin' to die. I heard her cryin' for an uncle of mine and he died the next day. He was sick at the time, but they didn't think he was goin' to die.[16]

In the Cootehall area of north Roscommon, it was recorded that 'the banshee follows a lot of people, Mac's and O's … and she cried around this part of the country not so long ago'.[17] Lysaght points out:

> Lean an bhean sí na fíor-Ghael uasal agus íseal agus an tslí a bhí ag na daoine chun an tuairim sin a nochtadh ná a rá gur lean sí na daoine go raibh 'Ó' nó 'Mac' ina sloinnte.

> [The banshee followed the true Irish nobility and commoner and the way people had of expressing that opinion was to say that she followed the people who had an 'O' or a 'Mac' in their name].[18]

One account from south Roscommon where the banshee was seen is interesting as a reflex of the well-known 'The Comb Legend' in which she is attacked while combing her hair.

> There was a dance this particular night in some village, and this bloke was livin' up in the mountain in a lonely place. He was coming to the dance, travelling alone and he carried a stick. On a mound or ditch he saw a little woman and she was combin' her hair, sittin' on the ditch. He let fly with th' ash plant or whatever he had and she disappeared. He didn't hit her, anyway. He come on to the dance and he told the crowd there what happened; that he saw the banshee. When the dance was over, your man was goin' home the mountain path again. The next mornin' he wasn't back. And they found him, with th' ash plant buried in his head, exactly in the place where he told this woman was.[19]

As Patricia Lysaght points out The Comb Legend warns about and teaches proper behaviour in dealing with supernatural beings:

> One should not accost another, least of all a defenceless woman. If it should transpire that the woman is a banshee or *badhb*, and is well able to defend herself, such aggressors will be properly punished.[20]

Some narrators described hearing the cry of the banshee close to a stream or river. One narrator from Tarmonbarry, a village on the Shannon, had heard from his uncle about an occasion when he and a neighbour were fishing for bream, about two o'clock in the morning:

> This morning they weren't long fishin' when the banshee came up to the side of the river. They were fishing from a boat. They took in the anchors immediately and began to pull for home as hard as they could. She followed them and they ran for the house and she after them, and she followed them as far as the big ash tree that was in the middle of the street.[21]

Another omen of death recorded in the River Shannon region is the dead/death coach or headless coach. Lysaght says concerning the dead coach:

> Ní fios fós ar lean na cóistí teaghlaigh áirithe mar ba nós leis an mbean sí. Ach bás daoine uasal, nó daoine mór le rá sa cheantar – tiarna talún b'fhéidir – a bhíonn i gceist go minic.

[It's not known yet whether the coaches followed certain families as was customary with the banshee. But it is the death of a noble person or someone of consequence –a landlord perhaps – that is at issue frequently].[22]

The connection of the dead coach with people of consequence is borne out in material from southwest Roscommon and northeast Galway.

Entrance to Mount Talbot

Two horses used to come down the Mount Talbot road from Mount Talbot House and down to the town of Athleague and a man with no head driving the carriage. It was a big black aul thing like the hearse that used to be goin' long ago. The horses were pullin' this aul' carriage. That Mount Talbot Road was always a bad spot.[23]

The coaches 'would also appear to be associated with certain roads, particularly roads to graveyards which would hint at a connection between the coaches and the old horse-drawn hearses'.[24] This is substantiated in material collected in south Roscommon.

The dead coach used to come to this corner here (i.e. to the cross at the Churchyard and Church of Clonown). Me brother was coming from a funeral in Taylorstown one night. This sidecar overtook him and there was two men on it and they took him up. But there was never a word spoken till he got out at this corner. The car disappeared after that.[25]

The Flynn family, who lived opposite the graveyard, claimed to have heard it many times. 'The dead coach was supposed to come in to our street here and turn on the street'. John Joe Flynn's explanation of the Dead Coach was that:

> People used be taken by the fairies long ago, and it seems they lived out their ordinary span of life among the fairies and then they died and they had to be buried. So they say that this dead coach was the hearse that used to be buryin' the people that died in the fairies.[26]

An explanation for the dead coach is found in material from Offaly:

> In them times anywhere there was a graveyard, there was body snatchers, "resurrectionists", they used to call them. If there was a funeral any place these lads would be watching and they'd come along that night with a hearse and they'd have a big grey pall over the horses' heads the way you'd think they had no head. And there'd be another cover over the driver's head. So the people would think, when they'd see the coach that it wasn't a right one. And they'd have the wheels muffled too, so that they would make no sound. The people used to guard the graves that time with scythes and pitchforks. It was done around here (i.e. body snatching). I knew people that remembered it being put down. It was made a criminal offence.[27]

Body snatching was quite common in the early years of the nineteenth century throughout Europe because anatomists paid well for bodies for scientific research. Thus the recently dead were watched over until such time as the corpse would no longer be of any use.

> At the close of the eighteenth century the country was infested with bands of resurrectionists, or "sack-em-ups," as they were indifferently called, who scrupled not to tear the peaceful dead from the graves and have them surreptitiously conveyed to the dissecting houses of the metropolis, for which they were amply compensated.[28]

William Talbot of Kilcormac, County Offaly, said the 'Resurrectionists' were common in his grandfather's time. 'He met this dead coach and seen it different times. He thought it was something supernatural. But it was only these Resurrectionists body-st'alin'. Ten pounds was the reward they got for a body'.[29]

It has been recorded frequently that if rigor mortis did not occur it was seen as a sign of another death in the family. 'If the corpse was limber it was taken as a sign that another member of the family would soon follow to the grave'.[30] The same belief has been recorded in English folklore: 'Most Cheshire people say a limber corpse is a sign of another death in a family shortly'.[31] Mary Anne Hanley, who was born in the townland of Kilbarry, County Roscommon, said that when her father died the man who shaved him said "it won't be long until someone else follows him", as the corpse had not stiffened. 'Sure enough me mother was dead within the fortnight. I remember too, that when me mother was in bed, the cock flew up on the window and crowed in at her'.[32] She also felt that bees swarming close to a house were a sign of bad luck. Before her husband died she had collected a swarm of bees which had come to her house. 'I was told at the time not to have anything to do with them, but I paid no heed'.[33] The belief that bees should be informed of a death is widely held. In the townland of Clooneigh, in east Roscommon, a family who kept bees always announced a death to the bees, otherwise they would leave the hive.[34] In Ballygar, northeast Galway also it was recorded that:

> When the head of a house dies, and there are bees kept, some person must go out and tell the bees. If this is not done the bees will leave. A man named McCormack had seventeen hives of bees, but when he died no one went out to tell the bees that he was dead. The day his corpse went up the *bóithrín* the bees followed him up and never went back.[35]

It was 'a common custom in Britain to 'inform' the bees when their master had died; the hives were struck three times with an old iron key and told of the death, sometimes in rhyme'.[36] Sharper Knowlson (author of *The Origins of Popular Superstitions and Customs*) referring to superstitions regarding bees and death points out that:

> The bee worked industriously and cleverly on behalf of the peasant, and asked no wages. In other words, the peasant was a debtor to the bee, and his attitude was one of gratitude. Out of this feeling, no doubt, arose a sense of identity in interests - a fellow-feeling which prompted him to "tell the bees" of a death, and to turn the hive at a burial.[37]

Death and Rites of Passage

At the time of death the material as well as the spiritual well being of the deceased was catered for to ensure a peaceful transition to the next life. Historian Ruth Richardson, referring to British death customs, points out that they appear remarkably tolerant towards the dead. 'This apparent tolerance derived not from any lack of fear but from an underlying belief that *due care of the dead* offered some assurance of the soul's future repose as well as providing comfort for the bereaved'.[38] Different rites served to separate the dead from the living, as the supernatural world was felt to be ever present. Van Gennep, the noted French ethnographer and folklorist, has subdivided *rites of passage* into *rites of separation, transition rites,* and *rites of incorporation.* The rites of separation from a previous world, which he calls 'preliminal rites', are prominent at the time of death, and he includes 'washings, anointings, and rites of purification in general', among the rites of separation.[39]

The desire for a peaceful and happy death led to various precautions being taken to ease the person who had difficulty dying. In different cultures anything that might contribute to what was referred to as a 'struggle with death' was removed if possible. Elsewhere in Europe, as in Ireland, it was customary to place the dying person on a straw mattress or straw on the floor. Reider Th. Christiansen, the distinguished Norwegian folklorist, has drawn attention to the fact that feathers were to be avoided, especially hens' feathers but also feathers of other birds (magpie, crow, birds of prey). It was believed in Norway that such birds carried a certain 'feather of unrest'. In Iceland 'the feathers of a grouse were held to be dangerous. Likewise in Germany, England, Ireland, Scotland and France, and the belief is even recorded from tribes in Russia'.[40] This is substantiated in interviews which James Delaney conducted throughout the midlands:

> There's a certain bed a man can't die on. They say that if there is a wild fowl's feather in the bed, a man can't die on it. So when anyone would be dyin' on a feather bed, they'd take them out of it.[41]

John Lennon of Kilmaccormac, County Roscommon gave the same reason: 'They wouldn't let them die on feathers in case there would be any wild bird's feather in it and they'd be in agony. The dying person was put out on the floor on straw'.[42]

Many of the narrators did not know of any particular reason for not allowing the person to die in a feather bed, other than that it eased the pain of death. 'They'd get it too hard to die on a feather bed, and that's why they used to take them out and put them on straw on the floor'.[43] In Mayo the reason given for removing a dying person from a feather bed was:

> Ar eagla go mbeadh clúmhach ins an leabaidh, a goideadh ná friothadh go héagcórach.
>
> [For fear there might be a feather in the bed that was stolen or strayed wrongly].[44]

In Estonia and Russia, Christiansen refers to the dying person being placed on 'a mattress filled with straw'.[45] The bed straw was burnt immediately the person had died, thus the neighbours were informed of the death. 'To the onlookers the most important part of the custom seems everywhere to have been the observation of the omen, obtained from the smoke. Its direction indicated the place from which the next funeral was to come'.[46]

A widespread custom was to wash or burn bedding and clothing which had been in contact with a corpse. In County Sligo, in the early nineteenth century, the practice was that 'as soon as the breath has departed from a sick person, the bed is carried out, and if there be high ground near the house, it is there set on fire and consumed to ashes, while the air resounds with doleful cries'.[47] Delaney recorded in the late 1950s, in Roscommon, 'long ago they used to have straw mattresses and the corpse was left out on this mattress, which was afterwards burned, after the funeral'.[48] He was also told that in 'olden days':

> They used to have a palliasse of straw with a feather tick over that. They used to burn the palliasse. In cases they didn't burn anything. It all depended on the disease the person died of.[49]

Christiansen says another reason for burning the bedding was 'due to a universal aversion against everything that had been in direct contact with a corpse.

The burning was generally performed without any special ceremony'.[50]

Before a person died the priest was sent for so that the last sacrament, Extreme Unction, could be administered. Traditionally people were advised to travel in pairs if they had to go on this errand, as they were felt to be vulnerable to attack from supernatural forces. Two lighted candles and a crucifix were placed on a table during the anointing. Members of the family and any others present gathered round the bed of the dying person to say the Rosary. 'The devotion of saying the Rosary was known in Ireland as early as the sixteenth century, if not in late medieval times'.[51] It was also customary to hold a blessed lighted candle or a crucifix, in the hand of the dying person. A custom which Ellen Hogan, of Four Roads near Roscommon town, said she had heard from her mother, nearly forty years earlier (i.e. than 1950s), was that the burial garment or 'habit' was used at the time of dying:

> When it is known that a person is going to die, the habit is bought, and the priest blesses it. This blessed habit should be used at the time of dying. The right arm of the dying person should be put in the right arm of the habit, at the same time that a lighted candle is held in the hand. The habit for men and married women is brown. Unmarried girls and children of Mary wear a white habit trimmed with blue ribbon. Some are members of the Third Order of St. Francis and these are left out in the brown habit of the Franciscan tertiaries.[52]

> The habit still used in places today, despite the inroads of secularism, is like a simply designed soutane (black) that sacristans and priests used to wear. The brown version may be of Carmelite origin. The male members of the Third Order (secular, as distinct from T. O. Regular) of St. Francis, at their profession, were given a brown habit like the ordinary Franciscan one, but without the capuche or hood. It is likely they were buried in it.[53]

In Ballymoe on the west Roscommon, east Galway border, it was recorded that people were laid out in 'a brown habit and brown stockings and gloves (brown) to represent the Brown Scapular of the Blessed Virgin Mary'.[54] It was customary in the midlands to leave the habit close to the person at the time of death. A narrator from northeast Galway said that old people believed:

That it would lighten the pains of purgatory, if they could put the hands of the person, who was about to die, in the sleeve of the habit, before they died. There was another old custom too. It doesn't matter if there was twenty women in the house, 'twas Mary always shook the Holy Water. That's one of the oldest customs now, from my grandmother. A person by the name of Mary must always shake the Holy Water, in honour of Our Lady, who is Mary.[55]

In most of the folklore accounts the right hand of the person was placed in the habit, although in some accounts it was the left hand.

Anyone who visited a house while a person was dying was expected to remain there until after the death. Everything was kept as quiet as possible and there were no outward displays of emotion. Pádraig Tyers, a Kerry author, says the desire for calm and quietness was because the dying person was said to have keen hearing. He also points out that:

Níor cheart gol mar go dtabharfadh san an duine tar nais agus go mbeadh sé ina sheiceadúir nó ina shiofróg gan crích gan aird an chuid eile dá shaol.

[It wasn't right to cry because that would bring the person back and he would be a useless and insignificant wretch for the rest of his life].[56]

'The corpse was both extremely vulnerable and extremely dangerous at or just after the moment of death. It had to be watched over but also guarded against'.[57] As J.G. Frazer, the eminent British anthropologist, pointed out:

There is an almost universal fear of the spirits of the dead. Man fears them because he feels instinctively that they are angels and ministers of death hovering about him in the air and ready to bear away his own soul with them to the unknown world beyond the grave.[58]

Prayers were said, candles were kept lighting, and holy water was sprinkled round the deathbed to guard against evil. It was a common custom to cover all polished surfaces or mirrors or to turn them to the wall.

This has variously been explained as a means of preventing the spirit of the dead person from seeing its own reflection and refusing to leave, and as a precaution lest the spirit take the reflection or double of any other person caught in the glass or other surface.[59]

It appears to have been an internationally observed custom to open doors and windows in order to give the spirit free passage. In modern Norway, 'when life had fled from the body, one opened the door just a crack. That way the soul would be free to go'.[60]

James Delaney and William Egan making a súgán

According to William Egan of Clonfanlough, County Offaly, immediately the person died, the window of the room was opened top and bottom because 'the angel used to come in overhead an' the devil had to go out under'. He had been given this explanation by a neighbour, who also believed that at the time of death space must be left beside the bed for the angel guardian.[61] These rituals of stopping clocks, covering mirrors and opening windows have been recorded throughout the midlands and they were observed until recently. In the parishes of Kilteevan, Tissrara and Kiltoom, in Roscommon, James Delaney recorded in the 1950s and 60s that doors and windows were opened, mirrors were covered and clocks were stopped.[62] Similar practices were recorded, in 1938, in the Ballymoe area. 'Clocks are stopped, mirrors are either taken from the room or turned into the wall'.[63] The reason given for stopping clocks was 'so that all could see the actual time of death, for which people usually made inquiry'.[64]

In northwest Roscommon, it was recorded that people who watched by a death-bed were very particular 'not to be in the way of the soul when it is leaving the room, and also any obstacle such as a set of knives, which may 'hurt' the soul, is removed from the passage through which it is believed it will depart'.[65] Some of the same practices and beliefs are attested internationally. Frazer has referred to a practice among the Basutos of South Africa when a native died, 'to make a hole in the thatch of the roof to let his soul go out by it, since the Basutos believe that the spirits of the dead cannot pass through openings used by living people'.[66] Christiansen said the practice of making a hole in the roof is also mentioned from Norway but 'one wonders if it was ever actually performed. The same idea – to speed the passage of the soul was expressed in a different way, when somebody climbed on to the roof and summoned the dying through the smoke hole'.[67] In many parts of Germany it was said to be customary after a death:

> to open doors and windows in order to let the soul fly away. In some parts of the Highlands of Scotland, the door of the room is left slightly ajar and in some parts of England at a death every bolt and lock in the house is unfastened.[68]

The latter practice was recorded in Clooneigh, in east Roscommon: 'When a person is dying the locks of everything in the house should be opened, locks on doors, boxes, trunks etc'.[69]

The dead person was left for three to four hours before being 'laid out', but they were never left alone. 'There were many reasons for this, principally respect and affection for the one who had died. There was also some degree of fear of supernatural intervention'.[70] A prayer book was placed beneath the chin or a cloth was tied round the deceased's head to keep the mouth closed. The limbs were composed, the arms were brought together over the breast and the hands were crossed. Ellen Hogan of Four Roads, County Roscommon, had heard older beliefs from her mother, nearly forty years earlier (i.e. c.1920): 'According to traditional belief, immediately the breath leaves the body the soul leaves the body also, but the soul is not judged till the corpse is washed'. The informant saw lights round her own home when her mother was dying. 'The old people said of those lights that come just as a person is dying, that they are the souls of the dying person's relatives, who come to take the soul away'.[71]

People took different measures to protect themselves against contagion as well as supernatural intervention at the time of death. In the east Mayo townland of Kilmovee, it was recorded:

Ní fhanann na daoine istigh fhaid a bhíos duine a fhágail bháis ar fhaitíos go dtóigfeadh siad an galar céadna go mór-mhór más é an eitinn a bhíos ag an duine.

[People wouldn't stay inside while a person was dying for fear that they would get the same illness especially if the person had tuberculosis].[72]

In other areas where this belief was recorded only relatives were in danger of contracting the disease so friends or neighbours remained until the person had died.

In the seventeenth century in Scotland any milk, onions or butter which happened to be in the house at the time of death were thrown away, as it was thought that in some manner the spirit would enter and corrupt them. In Brittany, butter was purposely placed on the table when a person died from cancer, in the belief that the disease would enter the butter which was afterwards taken outside and buried.[73]

Similar beliefs have been recorded in folklore in Roscommon and Sligo:

If there was any seed in a house and a person died in that house, then that seed that had lain in the house during the death would not be used. People wouldn't churn milk that had been gathered during a wake in the house.[74]

The reason given for not churning in County Sligo was:

If they were gathering milk for a churning that would not be kept: it wouldn't be churned. They claimed that the soul that was gone, might have come and dabbled with the milk. If there was a churning before the death, butter was made up in the house where the person had died; in little balls. No it wasn't eaten, it was just passed on and then stuck on the wall when the person passed out (died).[75]

James Currid, from near Sooey in south Sligo, explained what must be done with butter that had been churned:

> I've heard of the balls of butter being used at wakes; anyone that died with a contagious disease, consumption of decline, known as TB today. It was a fever, a disease, in the old days, because it wiped out families. There was always a ball of butter made up, and there was garlic in it. I've only heard of that, I've never seen it. They passed it along from hand to hand during the saying of The Rosary at the wake. I don't know what became of it afterwards: I think it was put in the coffin with the remains.[76]

In some of the accounts the milk was not used although the narrators did not know the reason, other than that it was the custom.

> Once the person dies any milk that's gathered is given to the pigs or left off in the strame. I seen milk that was gathered during a wake and it couldn't be et. It had to be thrown away after. Youngsters that didn't know the differ, gathered it and churned it. But it should never be used at all.[77]

All work ceased as soon as death was announced, and neighbours took over the chores that were absolutely necessary for the family of the deceased. It was customary for all the people of the village ('village' in the midlands means a group of dwellings in a townland) to suspend unnecessary farm work. John Kenny of Kiltoom, southeast Roscommon, illustrated it thus:

> If I am in the field now, ploughing with my horses, and somebody comes and says, "John, or Paddy so-and-so is dead", I take my horses from the plough immediately, and go home. That's the custom yet (i.e. 1960s).[78]

An account from northeast Galway was very similar:

> There was no work done in the whole village when there would be anyone over board. This custom is still carried out. Only necessary work is done but no one would think of yoking a horse to plough, for example.[79]

Preparing the Corpse
'The ritual treatment of the corpse prescribed by folk traditions guided families and friends through the painful separation of death'.[80] The rituals followed a set pattern and were adhered to as closely as possible out of a sense of respect as well as fear of the dead. It was

customary for three people to be involved in preparing the corpse; all three might not be directly involved but they would be present. As the twentieth century progressed the custom changed and two were often involved in laying out the dead and finally one. In the Parish of Cam, south Roscommon in the late 1950s:

> A handy woman in the neighbourhood left out the corpse, washed it and prepared it for the wake. She did it for men and women, but a man had to shave the corpse of a man, and not with a safety razor, either, but with an open razor.[81]

By the middle of the twentieth century traditions were changing and it was generally one particular person in an area who laid out the dead. It was recorded in 1958 in Athleague: 'It is very hard to get anyone to leave out a corpse nowadays'.(When Mrs. Ward's husband died three years previously (i.e. 1955) there was no one to lay him out and they had to send down to the Parish of Fuerty for a man to lay him out.)[82] On the Leitrim-Cavan border it was recorded that 'it is generally a relative living near, or a neighbour, who lays out a corpse. It's not like in some districts where the one person usually lays out all dead people'.[83] Those who laid out the corpse were relatives or neighbours of the deceased. In the Castlerea area of Roscommon, 'two neighbours, now, or friends, they'd be women, that'd lave out the corpse'.[84]

In the folklore accounts investigated, where the narrators were referring to the late nineteenth century and the early twentieth century, it was customary to have three people involved in laying out the corpse. In Kiltoom, southeast Roscommon, although John Kenny sometimes laid out a corpse with the help of another man, in earlier times the following was the custom:

> Three men usually leave out the men and three women leave out a woman. When leaving out a corpse we remove him from the bed to the floor. The washing is done on the floor and the corpse is washed completely from head to foot. The bed has to be removed altogether, then, mattress and all, and on the bed then we put a door and over the door we put a white sheet. (I suppose that's the reason they say "he's overboard", when they mean "he's wakin". Then we spread his habit on the bed and lift him in on to the habit. We put a beads (i.e. Rosary beads) between his fingers and a small crucifix.[85]

James Delaney and John Kenny

Mrs. Kate Ward of Athleague believed that the expression 'overboard' came from the time when 'the corpse was laid out in the kitchen on two tables, placed end to end'.[86] According to Ellen Hogan of Four Roads:

There should be three women to leave out a corpse and whether all three help in the work or not, they must be in the room, when the work is going on. Sometimes the help of a man is necessary to lift the remains in and out of the bed etc. a man's help was needed. The bed is stripped of its mattress and bed clothes. Instead of the mattress, a door or boards, are put on the bed, and the bed is then remade with two sheets and a quilt.[87]

The presence of three women is explained thus by Kathleen Hurley, a 1930s folklore recorder from Ballymoe: They 'represent the three Holy Women at the foot of the cross on Calvary and the three women at the tomb'.[88] Angela Partridge, Dept. of Modern Irish, University College Dublin, referring to 'na trí Mhuire' (the three Marys) says that clearly they are important:

luaitear iad chomh forleathan sin sa traidisiún béil agus tá go leor tagairtí dóibh sa litríocht scríofa.

[they are mentioned so widely in the oral tradition and there are many references to them in written literature].[89]

There were certain rituals observed in washing the body and in disposing of the water, soap and cloths used. As Wilson has pointed out 'water had an important role in its own right in purifying the corpse. Care had to be taken over the disposal of the water used to wash the corpse. In Transylvania, it had to be poured away, where no one will tread'.[90] The same procedures were recorded from the Irish midlands in the twentieth century. In the early material gathered in the 1930s, the dead body was left on clean straw or hay on the floor while it was being washed.

Soap and water and a wisp of hay are used for washing the body. When the washing is finished the wisps of hay which were used, are carefully gathered off the floor, and they together with the water in which the person was washed deposited somewhere, where no person or animal will walk over them.[91]

In Clooneigh the water used to wash the corpse was 'thrown out where it wouldn't be walked on'.[92] In Kiltoom, west of Athlone: 'The water was thrown under a whitethorn bush together with the cloth and soap. Cloth and soap could not be used again'.[93] It was recorded in Ballymoe that 'three squares of old worn linen' were used, and these were 'buried under a hedge in the garden as a mark of respect to the dead'.[94]

According to Mrs. Ward, who lived close to the Roscommon-Galway border, it wasn't customary to wash the whole body in Roscommon, although in some areas of the county it has been recorded that it was.

> Back in Galway they wash the corpse from the top of the head to the sole of the foot, but here (i.e. Athleague) they only wash the hands and feet and face. There was an old pisreóg that the dirt would be on them on the Day of Judgement, if they were not washed all over. The water is let down through a wall, where no one would trample on it. The basin, towel and soap were stuck someplace where they'll never be found, again. The razor was that is used to shave the dead man is also done away with.[95]

The soap which was used wasn't always discarded as it would have been regarded as wasteful to do so, according to some of the accounts recorded. In the material looked at, in all areas except Athleague and Kiltoom, the man who shaved the corpse kept the dead man's razor. There was usually one particular man who conducted this task and this remained the case until relatively recently.

It was customary to tie the two big toes of the corpse together to keep the legs straight, according to the folklore accounts. H. F. Feilberg, the Danish folklorist, describing burial practices in Denmark, gave the following reason:

> When the legs are tied together the dead cannot walk; the same thing when needles are run into the soles of the feet, it will cause pain to tread on them-also the fact that they are of steel has something to say in the matter.[96]

There is no mention of any other reason for tying the big toes together in the midlands other than simply to keep the feet together. The thumbs were sometimes tied with thread also, the tying being removed when the body was coffined. John Kenny, who laid out people in his own area, emphasized that 'no matter where I'd be myself, that person couldn't be coffined until I'd arrive to cut those twines. Nobody'd interfere with them only me'.[97] The tradition is widespread that those who prepare the corpse should be present to help with the coffining also. In all areas they were given a glass of whiskey for their work but no payment otherwise.

Laying out the Corpse
Henry Morris, who contributed many articles to folklore journals, described the corpse being laid out in the barn at the beginning of the twentieth century in Ulster:

> The barn was cleared out and a large table was placed at the end of the barn farthest from the door, and lengthwise on the floor. This table was covered with a sheet which hung down on all sides, and on the table was placed a plate containing clay pipes filled with tobacco, another plate full of teased tobacco, and a plate of snuff. There were also, in more recent times, a crucifix and some religious pictures placed at the head of the table. When the corpse was washed and dressed it was carried out to the barn and placed *under* the table, not on the floor but on a shelf, about eight or nine inches above the floor. (a door leaf or boards placed across the rails under the table formed an improvised shelf) In South Ulster, as well as in North Connacht, the corpse was always laid out in this fashion *under* the table: in Co. Donegal, on the other hand, the corpse was placed *on* the table.[98]

Pádraig Tyers, referring to customs in west Kerry, says it was *'faoi chlár an bhoird a bhíodh an corp sa tseanshaol'*. [Long ago the body used to be under the table].[99] Tyers described the deceased being laid out in the house but if a body was found in the sea or:

> an té a thabharfadh íde air féin ní scaoilfí a chorp isteach don tigh chun é a thórramh, ach cuirfí isteach i mbothán éigin lasmuigh é.

> [the body of a person who committed suicide would not be allowed into the house to be waked but would be put in a shed outside].[100]

At the end of the seventeenth century, Sir Henry Piers, a large landowner, described wakes in Westmeath thus: 'they sit commonly in a barn or large room and are entertained with beer and tobacco; the lights are set up on a table over the dead'.[101]

Scene at an Irish Wake.

Sketch of a wake from *Elder Faiths of Ireland* by Wakeman

There is no mention of the corpse being laid out under the table in the folklore collected by James Delaney. The only reference to the barn being used was in the case of a sudden death outside the house sometimes 'the body was not allowed into the house at all, but was waked in the barn'.[102] The barn was used only in exceptional circumstances, e.g. suicide or for the death of a stranger. These deaths were seen as unnatural, thus they could not be waked in the house as the living wished to guard themselves against restless spirits.

In the midlands the corpse was laid out on a table in the kitchen up to the 1920s according to information gathered in the 1930s, '50s and '60s. James Delaney recorded in 1960 that in Cam parish, south Roscommon, 'up to about fifty years or less, it was the general custom to have the corpse in the kitchen on a table'.[103] Later it changed to the bedroom, except in the case of older two roomed houses, where it was necessary to use the kitchen. 'In the mud hut and the daub house the remains were left "over board" on a table in the kitchen', according to information recorded in the Ballymoe area in 1938. The long table which was used was frequently borrowed as were the linen sheets and candle sticks.[104] Mrs. Annie Allen of Mount Temple, County Westmeath, whom James Delaney collected material from in the 1960s, remembered the corpse being laid out on the kitchen table.

> The feet of the corpse were always put facing the graveyard, where it was to be buried, either facing Castledaly or Mount Temple. Thus the position of the feet determined the corner of the kitchen in which the table was to be placed. Sheets were hung on thin rope or strong cord around the table and four sheets were used to form a canopy.[105]

Mrs. Annie Allen, age 97, holding her mother's towels (Sept 2008)

In investigating the material from the midlands this was the only reference to the position of the feet. Mrs. Allen retained linen sheets and towels, which had belonged to her mother which were used for laying out the dead. Sheets were made from home-grown flax in the nineteenth and early twentieth century and were often passed on from one generation to the next. Mrs Allen's sheets and towels were woven by an old weaver named Fox who lived in Cloonascra, north Offaly.

In all areas for which material was available, a canopy was formed by hanging sheets round the table or the bed. Accounts vary about the number of sheets used in laying out the corpse. In Clonown, south Roscommon, five sheets were used, four to form the canopy and the fifth was put over the corpse. 'Tucks were put in the front sheets and black bows were sewn on them'.[106] John Ledwidth of Moor parish, who remembered seeing a corpse laid out on the table described how the canopy was formed. 'They used to put up four standards and hang the sheets over the top of them and down the sides, and they'd leave the front open'. His sister-in-law told James Delaney that sheets were still used to form a canopy in the 1960s when the corpse was laid out on a bed.[107]

When the corpse was laid out on a bed it seems to have been common practice to use four sheets. Mrs. Kate Ward of Athleague emphasized that:

> Pure linen sheets were used. One sheet went under the corpse, one went over the back of the bed and another over the foot. They were draped over the head and foot. The fourth sheet was hung by the wall, alongside the corpse. The bed on which the corpse is laid out is tight against the wall. In old houses they are able to tie this fourth sheet up near the couples so that it hangs down the wall. A black bow is put on each side of the sheets and another in the centre-three black bows altogether.[108]

In all areas when beds were used a quilt was placed over the corpse which was folded back as far as the chest. It is still the practice to use a white quilt when the deceased is laid out at home. In Kiltoom, 'pieces of black crepe are put on the corners of the sheets. The crepe is tied into bows and pinned to the corners of the sheets'.[109] It was customary to use black crepe to decorate the sheets and sometimes a black cross of crepe was sown onto the top sheet or quilt. In Longford the following was recorded: 'The bed on which the corpse is laid out is always done up with sheets around it and laurel leaves pinned on the sheets in the form of a cross'.[110] Joseph Hanley of Clooneigh, who was 95 years old in 1958, described how

sally (willow) rods were used to make a canopy over the
bed.

> One sally rod made a bow over the head of the bed, and one
> made another bow at the foot. A third sally rod made a bow
> from head to foot, inside near the wall. The sheets were
> stretched over these bowed sally rods to make a canopy.[111]

The people who laid out the corpse had to take part in
the washing of the sheets also. This was usually done
three days after the death because it was believed,
according to Mrs. Allen, that 'it took the soul three days
to go to Heaven'.[112] Mrs. Kenny of Moor parish said that
'as a man always takes part in the leaving out of the
corpse, he also has to take part in the washing of the
sheets. But his part in the washing is only a token one.
He dips his hand into the water in which the sheets are
being washed'.[113] Thomas Kelly of Grange, south
Roscommon, described the ritual observed in washing
the sheets:

> Number one wrings out a sheet, hands it to Number Two,
> who wrings it also and then hands it to Number Three.
> Three wrings it, hands it back to Number One, who leaves it
> down.

Another custom he referred to was if a person died
outside the fire is quenched before the body is brought
in to be waked.[114]

Thomas Kelly with his grandnephew David Taylor
on his 90th birthday

Tom Harney and Tom Kelly, age 93 (August 2008)

Holy Water

Holy water (i.e. water that has been blessed by a priest) was always shaken round the room when a person was dying as it was felt that it protected against evil spirits. 'As Van Gennep has noted the burning candle, holy water, and prayers suggest the survival of ideas about the dangers of the first night after death for both the deceased and his family'.[115] After the corpse was laid out a small container with holy water was placed beside the body, with a little sprinkler fashioned of straw. It consisted of nine or ten straws cut to the same length of about eight inches: 'they were tied together with thread and used to sprinkle the holy water'.[116] The same custom was observed in France: 'A table next to the bed held a burning candle and a pitcher of holy water, which the guests would sprinkle on the dead with a branch of laurel or a palm preserved from Palm Sunday'.[117] The custom of having holy water in a small vessel with a sprinkler beside it was common in all parts of the midlands. People knelt down and said a prayer for the deceased and then they dipped the sprinkler in the holy water and shook it on the corpse. 'Everybody who goes in to see the corpse, sprinkles it with the holy water and says "Lord have mercy on poor John" etc'.[118] This practice has remained in use up to the present time when a person is laid out at home.

Candles

Candles have a symbolic as well as a ritual function and their use in connection with death is well documented. Candles were lit 'to protect the body from evil spirits and other dangers as well as to illuminate the deceased's journey to the other world'.[119] Blessed candles (blessed in a church on 2 February, the Feast of Candlemas) were used at the time of death and afterwards ordinary household candles were used according to information gathered in the midlands. It has been recorded that an uneven number were used; three or five was the general rule. 'The number of candles used always had to be an uneven number, usually either five or three, they are lighted immediately the corpse is "left out" and are kept lighting for the whole course of the wake'.[120] According to John Naughton and John Stroker from Kilteevan,

Roscommon, brass candlesticks were used and these would usually have to be borrowed, as most people had only two brass candlesticks. 'As soon as these borrowed candlesticks entered the house they were cleaned with ashes from the turf fire and a quenched coal (turf coal), as soon as they were brought into the house'. The two narrators did not agree about the number of candles, according to Delaney; one said five or seven while the other insisted it was six. It was explained later that John Stroker was getting confused with the number used in the church, which was six.[121] In Longford town a five branched brass candlestick was borrowed from the Cathedral, but Margaret Rogers from Aughintemple, reported that in her own district 'there was no borrowings from the church'.[122]

In practically all instances, according to the folklore accounts, an uneven number of candles was used- three or five. However some narrators described seeing even numbers of candles and they attributed different reasons: when 'the corpse was laid out on the table four or six candles were used. The candles were placed on the table, in a straight line on the inside, between the corpse and the wall'.[123] In describing wakes in parts of the north of Ireland, Henry Morris referred to 'five large candlesticks with candles, or in the case of those invested in the brown scapular, six candlesticks', placed on a small table at the foot of the corpse.[124] Two accounts from Westmeath described four candles being used; one narrator says they were placed at the head of the corpse while the other describes them as being placed at the foot of the corpse and that they were quenched during the day.[125] In north Roscommon, it was recorded in 1970, that 'generally two candles' were used at wakes in the 1930s, but this was later corrected by the narrator's sister-in-law who said it was 'five'.[126] Apart from the above accounts most of the folklore accounts stress the use of an uneven number of candles which were kept alight during the waking of the deceased.

The butts of the candles had cures associated with them, particularly the first candles that were lit.

> There is a cure in the wake candles, in the butts of the first
> candles used at the wake. The butts of these first candles are
> kept because there is a cure in them for the toothache. If you
> drop a drop of grease from the butt of one of these wake
> candles, on the affected tooth, it will cure the toothache.[127]

According to another source, if a person had a bad chest
cold or bronchitis, 'the butts of the candles should be
melted on to brown paper, and the brown paper should
be put on the chest'.[128] In Sligo also it was recorded that
'there's a cure in them for a weak chest, asthma, in the
grease of the candles that burns down the candlestick'.[129]
Ó Crualaoich, former Professor of Folklore at University
College Cork, refers to similar beliefs regarding the
curative properties in 'the stumps of candles burned by
the side of the corpse during the wake, for various
ailments such as swellings and burns, in the case of both
human and animal sufferers', as recorded in counties
Cork, Kerry and Mayo.[130] In some areas the butts were
placed in the coffin; 'As the candles die out, they are
collected and put in a paper till the body is coffined.
Then these candle butts are buried with the remains'.[131]
James Flynn of Clonown, south Roscommon, was not
sure what the cure was but a piece of a candle was sent
when returning anything borrowed for the wake. 'The
people that you'd get the sheets from, you'd have to
bring back a bit of the candle that was used at the wake.
Joe Roche of Taylorstown was tellin' me that lately'.[132] In
material recorded after the 1960s people were not aware
of any cures associated with the candles.

In some of the folklore accounts references are made
to a dish with salt being placed on or beside the corpse,
but there was no reason given for this custom:

> In the Highlands of Scotland in the mid eighteenth century,
> salt and earth were placed separately on a wooden platter
> on the breast of the deceased, the earth being seen as an
> emblem of the corruptible body; the salt of the immortal
> spirit.[133]

The late Estyn Evans, distinguished Professor of
Geography at Queen's University Belfast, who drew
extensively on folklore material in his research, has
written that 'a plate containing tobacco or salt was
placed on the corpse and sometimes a turf, which was
believed to prevent decomposition, a transference from
the observed preservative qualities of the bogs'.[134] He

does not mention where in Ireland this practice took place. No reference is made to earth being placed beside or on the body when the corpse was laid out in the material investigated for the midlands.

As soon as people heard of a death, after an interval of a few hours had elapsed to allow for laying out the corpse, they came to pay their respects. A special term was used for the house where the deceased reposed, and it was the same in all areas of the midlands:

> In the daytime the house where the dead person is, is called the "corpse house" or more usually "corp' house"; at night-from sunset to sunrise, the house is known as "the wake house".[135]

Notes

[1] A. & B. Rees, *Celtic Heritage: Ancient Tradition in Ireland and Wales*, London, 1961, 341.

[2] S. Wilson, *The Magical Universe Everyday Ritual and Magic in Pre-Modern Europe*, London 2000, 289.

[3] IFC 552: 274-275, collected by Kathleen Hurley, at Ballymoe, Co. Galway, 1938. Note: IFC refers to manuscript materials in the Irish Folklore Collection, in the Dept. of Irish Folklore, UCD.

[4] P. Bardan, *The Dead Watchers and other Folk-Lore Tales of Westmeath*, Mullingar 1891, 79.

[5] IFC 1573:18, collected by James Delaney from John Gately (Senior), Castletown, Curraghboy, Co. Roscommon, Sept, 1960.

[6] IFC 549:295-6, collected by Bríd Ní Ghamhnáin at Ballindoon, Boyle, Co. Roscommon, 1938.

[7] 1796:243-4, 309-11, collected by James Delaney from William Egan, Clonfanlough, Co. Offaly, January. 1970

[8] Lady Wilde, *Ancient Cures, Charms and Usages of Ireland*, London 1890, 60.

[9] IFC 1550:192, collected by James Delaney from Martin Nolan, Lissavruggy, Ballygar, Co. Galway, 1959.

[10] Patricia Lysaght, *The Banshee*, Dublin 1986, 193.

[11] Patricia Lysaght, 'An Bhean Sí sa Bhéaloideas', in B Ó Madagáin, ed., *Gnéithe Den Chaointeoireacht*, Baile Átha Cliath 1978, 53-66; 60.

[12] IFC 1677: 346, collected by James Delaney from John Connaughton, Lisduff, Co. Offaly, 1963.

[13] IFC 1526:137, collected by James Delaney from James Grady, Rinnegan, St John's, Co. Roscommon, December 1959.

[14] Lysaght, *The Banshee*, 61.

[15] IFC 1480:55, collected by James Delaney from James Flood, Ballinulty, Co. Longford, Sept.1957.

[16] IFC 1639:252, collected by James Delaney from Mrs. W. Kenny, America, Moor, Co. Roscommon, 1962.

[17] IFC 1781:247, collected by James Delaney from William Maxwell, Doorary, Cootehall, Co. Roscommon, 1970.

[18] Lysaght, 'An Bean Sí sa Bhéaloideas', 54.

[19] IFC 1575:73, collected by James Delaney from Thomas Kelly, Grange, Co. Roscommon, Sept. 1961.

[20] Lysaght, *The Banshee*, 179.

[21] IFC 1399:573, collected by James Delaney from James Neary, Ballytoohy, Tarmonbarry, Co. Roscommon, Aug. 1955.

[22] Patricia Lysaght, 'A Chóiste Gan Cheann Dén tAm San Oíche É', *Sinsear* 2 (1980), 43-59; 48.

[23] IFC 1526:386, collected by James Delaney from Mrs. Kate Ward, Corra More, Athleague, Co. Roscommon, 1959.

[24] Lysaght, 'A Chóiste Gan Cheann Dén tAm San Oíche É', 54.

[25] IFC 1575:132, collected by James Delaney from John Dunning, Clonown, Co. Roscommon, 1960.

[26] IFC 1575:284-5, collected by James Delaney from John Joe Flynn, Clonown, Co. Roscommon, 1960.

[27] IFC 1640:301, collected by James Delaney from William Talbot, Kilcormac, Co. Offaly, Nov. 1963.

[28] Bardan, *The Dead Watchers and other Folk-Lore Tales of Westmeath*, 78.

[29] IFC 1677:332, collected by James Delaney from William Talbot, Kilcormac, Co. Offaly, 1964.

[30] IFC 1487:75, collected by James Delaney from James Farrell, Furze, Lagan, Co. Longford, Oct. 1957.

[31] Christina Hole, 'Popular Modern Ideas on Folklore', *Folklore* 66 (1955), 321-9; 324.

[32] IFC 1550: 65, collected by James Delaney from Mary Anne Hanley, Derrymylan, Co. Roscommon, 1958.

[33] *Ibid.*, 318.

[34] IFC 1506:218, collected by James Delaney from John Stroker, Kilteevan, Co. Roscommon, 1958.

[35] IFC 1550:191, collected by James Delaney from Mrs Martin Nolan, Lissavruggy, Ballygar, Co. Galway, 1959.

[36] R.L. Brown, *A Book of Superstitions*, Newtown Abbot 1970, 98.

[37] T. Sharper Knowlson, *The Origins of Popular Superstitions and Customs*, London 1934, 207-210.

[38] Ruth Richardson, 'Death's Door: Thresholds and Boundaries in British Funeral Customs', Hilda E Richardson, ed., in *Boundaries and Thresholds*, Woodchester 1993, 91-102; 92.

[39] A. van Gennep, *The Rites of Passage*, paperback edn. London 1977, 146.

[40] Christiansen, 'The Dead and the Living', *Studia Norvegica* 2 (1946),24.

[41] IFC 1676:34, collected by James Delaney from John Purcell, Money, Kilcormac, Co. Offaly, 1963.

[42] IFC 1639:221, collected by James Delaney from John Lennon, Kilmaccormac, Co. Roscommon, Nov. 1962.

[43] IFC 1676:45, collected by James Delaney from Michael Shanny, Newtown, Kilcashel, Co. Roscommon, 1963.

[44] IFC 79:611, 'Pisreoga a bhaineas leis an mBás'.

[45] Christiansen, 'The Dead and the Living', 42.

[46] *Ibid.*, 26.

[47] W. Shaw Mason, *A Statistical Account or Parochial Survey of Ireland*, Dublin, 1814, 368.

[48] IFC 1550: 234-235, collected by James Delaney from Ellen Hogan, Four Roads, Co. Roscommon, 1959.

[49] IFC 1506: 218, collected by James Delaney from John Stroker, Kilteevan, Co. Roscommon, Spring, 1958.

[50] Christiansen, *The Dead and the Living*, 43.

[51] H. Fleming, 'A time of reform: from the 'penal laws' to the birth of Modern Nationalism' in B. Bradshaw & D. Keogh, eds., *Christianity in Ireland : Revisiting The Story*, Dublin 2002, 142.

[52] IFC 1550: 231, collected by James Delaney from Ellen Hogan, Four Roads, Co. Roscommon, 1959.

[53] Information received from Fr. Ignatius Fennessy, OFM, Franciscan Studies Centre, Killiney Co. Dublin, July 2003.

[54] IFC 552:304, collected by Kathleen Hurley at Ballymoe, Co.Galway, 1938.

[55] IFC 1550:277, collected by James Delaney from Michael Coughlan, Closhatoher, Co.Galway, 1959.

[56] P. Tyers, *Malairt Beatha*, Dún Chaoin 1992, 73.

[57] Wilson, *The Magical Universe*, 294.

[58] J.G.Frazer, *The Fear of the Dead in Primitive Religion*, London 1933, 40.

[59] Wilson, *The Magical Universe*, 294.

[60] *Ibid.*, 296.

[61] IFC 1796:14-15, collected by James Delaney from William Egan, Clonfanlough, County Offaly, May, 1970.

[62] IFC 1506:227 collected by James Delaney, from John Stroker, Kilteevan, Co. Roscommon, 1958; IFC 1550:233, from Ellen Hogan, Four Roads, Co. Roscommon, 1958; IFC 1639:268, from John Kenny, Newtown, Kiltoom, Co. Roscommon, 1962.

[63] IFC I552:304, collected by Kathleen Hurley, at Ballymoe, Co. Galway, 1938.

[64] K. Danagher, *In Ireland Long Ago*, Dublin 1964, 144.

[65] IFC 549:311, collected by Bríd Ní Ghamhnáin, at Ballindoon, Co. Roscommon, 1938.

[66] Frazer, *The Fear of the Dead in Primitive Religion*, 179.

[67] Christiansen, 'The Dead and the Living', 19.

[68] Frazer, *The Fear of the Dead in Primitive Religion*, 179-180.

[69] IFC 1507:60, collected by James Delaney from Joseph Hanley, Clooneigh, Co. Roscommon, May 1958.

[70] Danaher, *In Ireland Long Ago,* 144.

[71] IFC 1550:233, collected by James Delaney from Ellen Hogan, Four Roads, Co. Roscommon, Sept. 1959.

[72] IFC 194:53-5, collected by Pádraig Ó Ceannaigh from Pádraig Ó Reagáin, Cluain Fiachra, Cill Moibhí, Co. Mhaigh Eo, May 1935.

[73] B.S. Puckle, *Funeral Customs: Their Origin and Development,* reprint Detroit 1990, 111.

[74] IFC 1506:221, collected by James Delaney from John Stroker, Kilteevan, Co. Roscommon, 1958.

[75] IFC 1782:82-3, collected by Michael Murphy from Mrs. Joseph Meehan, Sooey, Co. Sligo, 1970.

[76] IFC 1782: 358-60, collected by Michael Murphy from James Currid, Shrananagh, Sooey, Co. Sligo, Feb. 1970.

[77] IFC 1575:505-6, collected by James Delaney from Kieran Mc Manus, Nure, Co. Roscommon, Feb. 1962.

[78] IFC 1639:268, collected by James Delaney from John Kenny, Newtown, Kiltoom, Co. Roscommon, 1962.

[79] IFC 1550:212, collected by James Delaney from John Noone, Kilclough, Ballinasloe, Co. Galway, Sept. 1959.

[80] T.A. Kselman, *Death and the Afterlife in Modern France,* Princeton 1993, 55.

[81] IFC 1550:166, collected by James Delaney from Patrick Mac Donnell, Caltra, Co. Roscommon, 1958.

[82] IFC 1506:531, collected by James Delaney from Mrs. Kate Ward, Athleague, Co. Roscommon, Summer 1958. (note from collector)

[83] IFC 1507:174, collected by James Delaney from Patrick Mc Govern, Swanlinbar, Co. Cavan, 1958.

[84] IFC 1736:218-9, collected by James Delaney from William Rourke, Cloonkeen, Castlerea, Co. Roscommon, Nov. 1966.

[85] IFC 1639:234, collected by James Delaney from John Kenny, Newtown, Kiltoom, Co. Roscommon, 1964.

[86] IFC 15 collected by James Delaney from Mrs. Kate Ward, Athleague, Co. Roscommon, Summer 1958.

[87] IFC 1550:234, collected by James Delaney from Ellen Hogan, Four Roads, Co. Roscommon, 1959.

[88] IFC 552:303, collected by Kathleen Hurley at Ballymoe, Co. Galway, 1938.

[89] Angela Partridge, *Caoineadh na dTrí Muire,* Baile Átha Cliath 1983, 106.

[90] Wilson, *The Magical Universe,* 295.

[91] IFC 549:314, collected by Bríd Ní Ghamhnáin, at Ballindoon, Co. Roscommon, 1938.

[92] IFC 1506:250, collected by James Delaney from Joseph Hanley, Clooneigh, Co. Roscommon, 1958.

93 IFC 1639:236, collected by James Delaney from John Kenny, Newtown, Kiltoom, Co. Roscommon, 1962.

94 IFC 552:305, collected by Kathleen Hurley, at Ballymoe, Co. Galway.

95 IFC 1506:531-532, collected by James Delaney from Mrs. Kate Ward, Corramore, Athleague, Co. Roscommon, May 1958.

96 H F Feilberg, 'The Corpse-Door: A Danish Survival', *Folk-Lore*, 18, London (1907) 362-375; 368.

97 IFC 1781:422, collected by James Delaney from John Kenny, Newtown, Kiltoom, Co. Roscommon, 1970.

98 H. Morris, 'Irish Wake Games', *Béaloideas*, 8 (1938), 123-41; 127-8.

99 Tyers, *Malairt Beatha*, 84.

100 *Ibid.*, 84-6.

101 H. Piers, 'A Chorographical Description of the County of Westmeath 1682', C. Vallancey, in *Collectanea de Rebus Hibernicis*, 1 Dublin 1682, 1-126;124.

102 IFC 1640:33, collected by James Delaney from Thomas Kelly, Grange, Co. Roscommon, 1963.

103 IFC 1551:389, collected by James Delaney from John Gately, Castletown, Curraghboy, Co. Roscommon, February 1960.

104 IFC 552:306, collected by Kathleen Hurley, at Ballymoe, Co.Galway, 1938.

105 IFC 1771:342-344, collected by James Delaney from Mrs. Allen, Mount Temple, Co. Westmeath, Sept. 1968.

106 IFC 1575:445, collected by James Delaney from James Flynn, Clonown, Co. Roscommon, Jan. 1962.

107 IFC 1639:166, collected by James Delaney from John Ledwidth, America, Moor, Co. Roscommon, Spring 1962.

108 IFC 1506:532-533, collected by James Delaney from Mrs. Kathleen Ward, Corramore, Athleague, Co. Roscommon, June 1958.

109 IFC 1639:235, collected by James Delaney from John Kenny, Newtown, Kiltoom, Co. Roscommon, 1962.

110 IFC 1487:409, collected by James Delaney from Eugene Clarke and James Nolan, Ohill, Co. Longford, Dec. 1957

111 IFC 1507: 68, collected by James Delaney from Joseph Hanley, Clooneigh, Fourmile House, Co. Roscommon, 1958.

112 IFC 1771:342-346, collected by James Delaney from Mrs. Allen, Mount Temple, Co. Roscommon, 1967.

113 IFC 1639:391-392, collected by James Delaney from Mrs Kenny, America, Moor, Co. Roscommon, 1963.

114 IFC 1640:32-33, collected by James Delaney from Thomas Kelly, Grange, Co. Roscommon, 1963.

115 Kselman, *Death and the Afterlife in Modern France*, Princeton, 1993, 52.

116 IFC 1781:423-424, collected by James Delaney from John Kenny, Newtown, Kiltoom Co. Roscommon, 1970.

117 Kselman, *Death and the Afterlife in Modern France*, 51.

[118] IFC 1526:95, collected by James Delaney from James Grady, Rinnegan, St. John's, Co. Roscommon, Dec. 1959.

[119] Wilson, *The Magical Universe*, 294.

[120] IFC 1550:236, collected by James Delaney from Ellen Hogan, Four Roads, Co. Roscommon, Sept. 1958.

[121] IFC 1506:227, 240, collected by James Delaney from John Naughton and John Stroker of Kilteevan, Co. Roscommon, 1958.

[122] IFC 1399:652, collected by James Delaney from Margaret Rogers, Aughintemple, Co. Longford, August, 1955

[123] IFC 1551:390, collected by James Delaney from John Gately, Castletown, Curraghboy, Co Roscommon, Feb.1960.

[124] Morris, 'Irish Wake Games', 128.

[125] IFC 1771:344, collected by James Delaney from Mrs. Allen, Mount Temple, Co. Westmeath, 1967; IFC 1736:30, collected from Patrick Doolin, Coolruck, Ballykieran, Co. Westmeath, Dec. 1966.

[126] IFC 1781:29,88, collected by James Delaney from James Maxwell, Cootehall, Co. Roscommon, 1970.

[127] IFC 1487:409, collected by James Delaney from Eugene Clarke and James Nolan, Ohill, Killoe, Co. Longford, Dec. 1957.

[128] IFC 1550:67, collected by James Delaney from Mrs. Anne Hanley, Derraghmylan, Rooskey , Co. Roscommon, 1959.

[129] IFC 1782:88, recorded by Michael Murphy from Mrs. Meehan, Sooey, Co. Sligo, 1970.

[130] G. Ó Crualaoich, 'The Production and Consumption of Sacred Substances in Irish Funerary Tradition', H. Pekka Huttunen & R. Latvio, eds., in Entering The Arena: Presenting Celtic Studies in Finland, *Etiainen* 2, Turku 1993, 39-51; 43.

[131] IFC 1550:236, collected by James Delaney from Ellen Hogan, Four Roads, Co. Roscommon Sept. 1958.

[132] IFC 1575:446, collected by James Delaney from James Flynn, Clonown, Co. Roscommon, Jan. 1962.

[133] Wilson, *The Magical Universe*, 295.

[134] E. Evans, *Irish Folk Ways*, London 1972, 290.

[135] IFC 1506:219-20, collected by James Delaney from John Stroker, Kilteevan, Co. Roscommon, Spring 1958.

Chapter Two

The Wake

> The custom of waking or watching originated with the Irish
> in an affectionate feeling towards their dead relatives,
> whom their natural kindness prompted them not to desert,
> as it were, nor to leave to the attacks of evil spirits who
> hover in their fancy round the body to do it an injury.[1]

Wakes were social occasions; games, storytelling, eating,
drinking and smoking were all features of the wake. As
Seán Ó Súilleabháin, the distinguished Irish folklorist,
points out, Ireland was not unique in these practices.
'They were all part of a widespread common pattern of
popular custom throughout Europe, in Iceland and
elsewhere'.[2] The whole tone of the wake however
depended upon the circumstances of the death. If a
young person had died there was genuine sorrow and
the wake was a sombre occasion but if it was an older
person the event was more of a social occasion, and was
looked forward to particularly by young people. The
social aspect of the wake and its importance in the local
community in earlier times was evident in an account
from the Ballinamuck area of Longford. The narrator's
mother had heard from his great grandmother that:

> They were short of wakes one time in Gelsha, and there was
> an auld fellow named Begley, a piper, pretended to be dead
> so that he'd have a wake. The piper had the pipes in the bed
> with him and suddenly he began to tune the pipes. The
> crowd cleared.[3]

Lysaght suggests that:

> The two key elements of the wake – lamenting and revelry –
> correspond to the universal features of the funeral rites of
> traditional cultures identified in van Gennep's analysis of
> passage ritual, namely public mourning and a period of
> licence.[4]

The wake usually lasted two nights but this depended
on the time the person died. In Mount Temple, County
Westmeath, according to James Flynn, who was 84 years:
'In aul' times there was always two nights wake. But

that's all done away with now (i.e 1967)'. Later in the interview he points out that 'if a person died about eleven o'clock at night, there'd be hardly any wake that night. But there'd be a big wake the next night and big crowds of people'.[5] Folklore accounts show that people's recollections of the customs and procedures were very similar throughout the midlands.

Preparations for the Wake

It was customary for three people to go for the requisites for the wake, usually a family member and two neighbours or friends or sometimes those who laid out the body. According to James Delaney, in some places:

> The requisites for the wake and funeral are called "funeral charges", and there were well established rules governing the whole business, as regards the number of people to be sent, what they must buy and even that they were expected to have a meal in the town etc.[6]

There was some variation between areas in how the requirements were described, who went to get them and whether women were involved. In Castlerea, it was called 'going for the buryin', and 'they went on an ass and cart or a horse and cart, whatever they had'.[7] In Ballymoe, 'three men–a member of the family of the deceased, a relation and a neighbour go into town for the burial charges'.[8] The importance of three going was emphasized in all the folklore accounts and they went to the nearest town: 'The nearest relatives went for the supplies for the wake. If the mother died, the father and son and an uncle of the son would go. Three men went as a rule for the supplies and never less than three'.[9] In all the folklore investigated the number was always three and as a general rule it was men who went. In Athleague, 'It is always three men who go for the "burying charges" and always neighbours. No woman ever went for the burying charges'.[10] The parishes of Moor and Drum were the only places James Delaney said he ever heard 'of the custom of a woman accompanying the three men to town for the funeral expenses. In other areas it was generally three men who did this'.[11] Kieran Mc Manus of Nure (Drum Parish) told James Delaney 'they always bring a woman or a girl with them from the house in which the death occurs, and she'd be master over the groceries'.[12] This is substantiated by Edward Egan: His father would always say 'there's someone dead in Nure, or somebody died in Drumlosh, when he saw two men and a woman in the middle passing at a quick pace in a horse and cart'.[13] In Moor, according to John Ledwidth, 'two men usually go for "the funeral expenses" and they always bring a woman with them'. Mrs. Ledwidth said in relation to the custom of bringing a woman for the funeral expenses, that it was an old custom. The requisites for the wake were always written out for the men by a woman, so although women did not generally accompany the men they were involved.[14]

In south Roscommon it was recorded that it was customary not to pay for the requisites until after the burial:

> Sugar, tea, bread, jam etc. are the main items in the funeral expenses and whiskey. Candles also have to be bought. Three have to go for the funeral expenses. Usually the three men that leave out the corpse (if a man had died) go to town for the funeral expenses. You should never pay for the funeral expenses on the day that you'd go for them.[15]

James Farrell of Lagan, Longford, told about a man who took advantage of the custom, and ordered drink and other things for his father's wake in Longford:

> At that time when you'd go into a shop to buy the funeral stuff, you'd never be asked for money. You'd get it all on tick. In about a month after who landed into Kelly's only the father. He was mad alive. Kelly got the surprise of his life.[16]

In the folklore accounts investigated, the customs in the midlands are similar but differences are apparent in the terms used for the requisites for the wake in the different counties. In Kilcormac, County Offaly, the following was recorded:

> Funeral arrangements is the term applied to the business of buying things for the wake and funeral. It is usual for two people to go to Kilcormac to see about the arrangements. Fifty years ago they'd bring home gallons of whiskey, pipes, tobacco and snuff. They would also bring wine and minerals, bread, butter, jam and candles. There was no porter at the wakes in those times. Nowadays, however it is customary to have bottled stout at wakes.[17]

In the parish of Ballinahown, on the Offaly-Westmeath border, 'two men and probably a woman with them would go to Athlone for the things for the wake and funeral'. The narrator did not know any particular name for the requisites except that 'long ago they used to bring the coffin home with them in the cart, along with the food, drink, pipes, tobacco and snuff'.[18]

The requirements for the wake were the same in all the accounts - candles, clay pipes, tobacco, snuff, tea, sugar, bread, jam, whiskey, wine and porter. In earlier times the timber for making the coffin was also acquired.

> At that time (fifty years ago) when they'd be buyin' the burial charges they'd buy the makings of the coffin for about seven shillings. They'd buy about ten or twelve dozen pipes, and two or three pounds of tobacco, and snuff, and other kinds of drink, besides porter, like wine.[19]

In the early folklore accounts tea, bread and butter, and jam was the usual fare for wakes. Later, when people could afford it, ham, cheese, cake and biscuits were introduced. In northwest Roscommon 'in olden times people who could afford it, often gave meat but seldom this is done nowadays, except in the case of a Protestant wake, then occasionally there is meat given'.[20] According to folklore collected on the Leitrim-Cavan border, 'it wasn't customary to buy meat', with the other supplies for the wake.[21]

Coffin

The French social historian, Philippe Ariès points out that after the thirteenth century in Latin Christendom:

> The body of the deceased was sewn into a shroud from head to foot and then often enclosed in a wooden chest or coffin. People who were too poor to pay the carpenter were carried to the cemetery in a common coffin designed only for transport.[22]

The origin of coffins can be traced to an attempt to preserve the corpse as long as possible from decay. The body wrapped in a shroud and placed directly in the ground is:

> an ancient practice that persists to this day in Islamic countries. In the medieval West there seems to have been an aversion to this bareness. It was then that the bier that

served for transport was transformed into a closed wooden chest, the sarceu.[23]

Throughout Europe the poor who could not afford coffins were often just buried in a winding sheet.

> In early days in England the bodies of the poor were committed to the grave practically naked, or at best wrapped in a shroud of linen, and only the prosperous were allowed to be "chested," as it was called. In the year 1666 an Act came into force insisting that all persons should be buried in a shroud composed of woollen material in place of linen previously used.[24]

In some parts of Donegal coffins came into use only at the beginning of the twentieth century according to information received from Donegal by Ó Cinnéide.

> Deir Conallaigh liom nách rófhada coirp á n-adlacadh i gcónraí agus nách mó tuairim cheithre fichid bliain ann ó thugtaí an corp chun na reilige sínte ar chómhla dorais agus taiséide dhearg á chumhdach.

> [Donegal men told me that it is not so long since the corpse has been buried in a coffin and that it is not more than about eighty years since the corpse was brought to the graveyard lying on a door leaf wrapped in a red shroud.][25]

It was customary in the midlands, in the late nineteenth and early twentieth centuries, to buy the timber for the coffin and have a carpenter or handyman make it. In some of the folklore accounts, where the narrators were referring to the Famine, people were buried without a coffin or else in wicker coffins.

> It had a false bottom in it and they could let this bottom fall out and the corpse would be buried without e'er a coffin. I heard me father and grandfather talkin' about the Famine. I seen me grandfather here and remember him. He was eighty six when he died, and I was about six years auld at that time. [This would mean that his grandfather was born in 1794 and would have been fifty two years old at the time of the Famine of '46].[26]

In north Offaly during the Famine, 'they got so pushed then for coffins, they used to bury them without a coffin. They'd bring the corpse in this aul' basket and bury the corpse without any coffin, and bring back the basket for the next one'.[27] In Sligo, the narrator's grandfather had seen wicker coffins made:

He lived to be ninety two or three years, he told me how these coffins were made with sally rods. They worked from the centre of the body, I suppose; up to the head and down to the feet. That was the two-tier one for a big tall man. And then they barrelled it in: I seen the 'barrelling' done myself on creels: widened it out when they came on to the shoulders, and then they narrowed it in again after that. At the top and bottom of the coffin they platted them together, and they tied them in with another rod round the top.[28]

Alan Gailey, former Director of the Ulster Folk and Transport Museum, referred to information submitted to the Museum from Michael Murphy, folklore collector, describing the remains of a wicker coffin, from Ballysheil Graveyard, found at a funeral in 1968. His description of how he thought it would have been constructed is very similar to the example from Sligo.[29]

At the end of the nineteenth century and the beginning of the twentieth the boards for the coffin, a few lengths of white deal, were bought with the other requirements for the wake. Later when ready-made coffins became available they were bought and brought home on a horse and cart. 'One of the principal items was boards of white deal, with which to make the coffin. Some sort of black material called shrouding was also bought to cover the outside of the coffin'.[30] The older narrators' accounts are practically all the same as regards the timber for the coffin. 'They'd buy the boards for about fifteen shillings when they'd be buyin' the burying things', according to John Gately of Coolagarry, County Roscommon, who was 85yrs old in 1960.[31] It was the same procedure in south Longford:

When they'd go to the town for the funeral charges they also got a couple of twelve foot dale boards to make the coffin. In my young days you wouldn't get a coffin to buy like now. It had to be made by the local carpenter or some handy fellow would make it. Nowadays (i.e. 1957) it is twenty two pounds for an oak coffin, the grandest coffin ever you seen.[32]

Accounts varied about when the coffin was made; most remembered it being made at night-time, either on the first or second night. 'The coffin was always made after dark in them times on the second night, the night before the burial day. There would be a couple of men at the makin' of it, maybe more, but there would be two anyhow'.[33] Generally the timing seemed to depend on when the person died and whoever was making the coffin.

> They'd bring the carpenter to the house and he'd make it in the barn. He might spend a while at it during the night, when he'd come to the wake, but it was generally during the daytime that he worked at it. It was painted and varnished and looked very well.[34]

If the family of the deceased did not have a barn or the corpse was being waked in the barn, it was made in a neighbour's barn. Michael Coughlan of Closhatoher, northeast Galway remembered his grandfather's coffin being made in a neighbour's barn. It was made by Mike Conroy in Patch Ward's barn in Rushinstown.

> The coffin was a simple affair. There were two full boards for the sides and two ends nailed on to the head and foot. The bottom was a series of small boards nailed across, beside one another. The lid was two full pieces joined together, with two pieces added on for the shoulders. Three saw cuts or kerfs were made across the side boards, in order to enable the carpenter to bend the boards at the shoulder and that was the only piece that gave any difficulty in the making.[35]

The earlier coffins were covered with black cloth which was tacked on with black, round headed tacks. 'If the person dead were young, the coffin was covered with a white material. For children it would be a white linen covering with a blue cross made of blue ribbon'.[36] A description from County Longford was similar:

> The coffin was covered with black stuff, they called black shroudin'. That was for a grown up person, but if it was for a youngster they were makin' the coffin, they'd use white stuff to cover it. There was no linin' inside the coffin, only the bare boards.[37]

In northwest Roscommon it was recorded in the late 1930s that:

> Coffins nowadays are always bought at the Undertakers, but in olden times people themselves had to supply them. A neighbouring handyman, or the local carpenter usually made it, and an old custom was that the people who were getting it made were never charged any money for the work.[38]

The same custom was recorded in the Mount Talbot area of southwest Roscommon. James Nolan's father used to make coffins for the neighbourhood and then the task passed on to James himself. 'I made hundreds of coffins in me time and never got as much as a copper for the makin' of them. We never charged for makin' coffins, nayther me father or meself'.[39] The general rule was that the carpenter did not charge for making the coffin but he was given whiskey. James Flynn of Mount Temple, County Westmeath, never saw a coffin being made at the house where the wake was held but otherwise his account is similar: 'Balfe from Mount Temple used to make the coffins. He never charged for makin' them. All you had to do was bring him the boards and he'd make the coffin for nothing'.[40] William Maxwell of Doogary, Boyle, saw a coffin being made only once and said 'it was made in the house: a black coffin it was, painted black'.[41]

The mountings for the coffin, i.e. breastplate, handles etc., were bought with the boards. 'If they had no mountings on the coffin the people would say it was a Poor House coffin. The poor house coffin had no mountings and was yellow in colour'.[42] Most of the narrators refer to the breastplate being bought with the timber for the coffin. 'It was usually made of tin, with black paint coverin' it. Then some handy man would paint on the name of the dead person, the age, and the date of death'.[43] It has been recorded in Galway that the correct age was never put on a breastplate. 'The person was always made out to be younger, by three or four years or more'.[44] The same custom was common in other areas and continued until relatively recently.[45]

According to Kathleen Hurley of Ballymoe:

Prior to the year 1911 coffins varied in make, colour and fittings. From about 1911 all coffins whether they be for the young, persons in middle or advanced years, are painted oak colour. At the present time, 1938, coffins are sold in shops in the towns.[46]

In Castlerea, William Rourke could date the first of the shop coffins: 'Me mother's coffin was the first of them (i.e. shop coffins) that ever came round our side'. His mother had died about sixty years previously, and the coffin cost two pounds.[47] Murray's in Knockcroghery sold habits and coffins and Emmet Murray, referring to wakes in the 1920s and 1930s, said that the preparation of the coffin was a specialized job.

Mrs. Anne Murray

The mountings had to be nailed to the sides and the coffin lined with satin and purple tassels on the top. The breastplate was inscribed by my mother and she could not be disturbed when she was doing this as it was a work of art. As children we were very proud of her beautiful writing.[48]

Keening

The tradition of keening at wakes was observed in the midlands until the beginning of the twentieth century. According to the material investigated the custom of keening the body on the journey to the graveyard and at the burial continued later in the century.

> In coming into the presence of the corpse after all the preparations were completed, the mourners gathered round the body and lamented for the first time. By so doing they signalled the commencement of the wake.[49]

According to Professor Seamus Ó Catháin, of the School of Irish Celtic Studies, Irish Folklore and Linguistics at University College Dublin, the tradition of keening is very old and can be traced back in early writings:

> Is sa Ghréig atá na caointe is sine le fáil: tá caoineadh le fáil san Iliad féin agus insíonn Arastotail dúinn go gcaithfear idirdhealú a dhéanamh idir threnos (aon cheoltóir amháin) agus an caoineadh dramáta kommós atá bunaithe ar cheol ainteafanúil. Bhí an caoineadh le fáil freisin sa 17ú agus san 18ú haois i Sasana agus in Albain agus suas go dtí le gairid inár dtír féin.

> [In Greece the oldest form of keening is found: keening is to be found in the Iliad itself and Aristotle tells us that a distinction must be made between threnos (one musician only) and the dramatic keening kommós that is based on antiphonal music. Keening was to be found also in the 17th and 18th centuries in England and Scotland and up to recently in our own country].[50]

In folklore gathered in 1938 in northwest Roscommon the following description of keeners can be found:

> Long ago special "keeners" were employed to cry for the dead. They were usually old women, and they came specially dressed for the occasion. They usually shook ashes in their hair, and wore shoes that had not been cleaned for weeks before the funeral, sometimes too, they appeared in their bare feet.[51]

John Connaughton of Lisduff, County Offaly, remembered seeing keeners at his grandfather's wake:

He lived beyond the Shannon there in Clonfert and I was only a gossoon at the time and I went over with me father and mother. The corpse was left out in the room. And they'd raise this cry when any of the friends would come into the room where the corpse was. They'd keen over the corpse. Any friend (i.e. relative) that was after coming a bit of a distance at all, they'd raise this cry when she'd come into the corpse room and the woman that'd come in would join in with them.[52]

John Connaughton, family, neighbours and James Delaney

The tradition of keening at the wake seems to have died out since the end of the second half of the nineteenth century in Roscommon. In the Parish of Taughmaconnell it was recorded:

The last time I seen them cryin', it was over Nancy Galvin and the aul' man, her husband, was cryin', out loud and clappin' his hands and cryin', 'Woe! Woe! Woe! That was in 1893 that Nancy Galvin was dead. They used to cry at wakes in them times, too. At me mother's funeral in '95 there was no cryin'. But I heard them cryin' at wakes in my time. It quit about fifty years ago, but it finished at funerals in '93 at Galvins.[53]

The older narrators knew the format the keening took, although they may not have witnessed it themselves. Thomas Horan of Ballyduff, Co. Offaly, who was 82 years of age, described keening when he was young:

> The women, at the wake, used to go up to the room, where the corpse was every two or three hours, and cry over the corpse. They used no words, but it was a kind of chant. There was an aul' w'aver in the parish and he was a great crier.[54]

When James Delaney recorded John Kenny in the 1960s he said his grandfather had died in 1921, aged 92, and he never heard him mention anything about the custom. However, according to Delaney, 'the tradition of keening or crying for the dead at wakes and funerals is very strong in other parts of South Roscommon and the custom was observed within living memory in Drum and other parts of the county'.[55] Keening went on up to 1950 in Nure, according to Edward Egan, 'not in the houses but after the hearse went out; Pak Mc Manus when he died, his sister Ellie keened out for two hundred yards out the road'.[56] The material investigated shows that keening took place at the same periods of time identified by Lysaght. 'The main phases of lamentation occurred during the wake and funeral – that critical period during which the deceased remains among the living'.[57]

Attendance at the Wake

> The Irish considered attendance at the wake one of the principal obligations of religion and followed an established series of intensely emotional phases of weeping, joking, insulting the cadaver, drinking and eating.[58]

The wake was not just an occasion for overindulgence; attendance demonstrated a sense of obligation to the living as well as affection and respect for the dead. 'The people of the house are never left to themselves for the whole course of the wake. This is a very strict rule, that some neighbours (or neighbour) must always keep the family company, while the corpse is in the house'.[59] It was also the practice in other European countries not to leave the family alone with the corpse, from the time of death to interment.

During the first night after death, sometimes on the last before interment, or even on all nights between, it was the duty of friends and neighbours to honour the deceased with their company. Such wakes, vigilia, have been held in most European countries and are in some still in use.[60]

Accounts vary about who attended the wake; generally it was young people at night-time although in some areas of Roscommon young women were prohibited from attending wakes. 'Big crowds used to be at wakes fifty and sixty years ago. The women and aul' men all went to the corp' house. I never seen any childer at a corp' house or a wake. It was all young men would be at a wake'.[61] In other areas of south Roscommon it was customary for everyone to attend the wake, although young children would usually be sent to a neighbour's house.

Everyone attended the wake at night, men and women, boys and girls, young and old. The priests were again young women attending wakes, one time, here, but they kept goin' whether the priests liked it or not. There used to be very big wakes in aul' times and they do have them yet.[62]

An account from Offaly is similar:

I heard the priest sayin' that no one was to go to a wake at all, unless they were near friends of the dead person. I heard the priest readin' it out. But the people passed no remarks on it. In them times they used to go miles to a wake and every wake would be full.[63]

Often there was not enough room for everyone who attended in the wake house, as the traditional houses were two or three roomed, so the barn was used by the younger people for dancing and games. This was done for convenience rather than a reluctance to carry on with such festivities in the presence of the corpse. In Westmeath it was recorded that 'aul people and relatives of the deceased person would be in the house. The young people would be all in the barn. Young women used to be at wakes and some of them would be in the barn. That would be before 1906'.[64] As Ó Suilleabháin points out 'the great occasion was in honour of the deceased alone, and he was the only guest'.[65] An acceptance of this fact helps one to understand some of the practices of the wake which many commentators found objectionable. Christiansen points out that originally the wake was a social not a religious event.

'With a kind of intensified exaggeration the deceased is treated, not only as one being still alive, but as the centre of many activities, before he finally retreats from the scene'.[66]

In the Parish of St. John's, near Athlone: 'The young men generally gathered in to the wake about nine or ten o'clock, when the old people would be slipping away home. Young unmarried girls could go to the corp' house, but not to the wake'.[67] According to folklore collected in the late 1950s:

> This prohibition on young unmarried women came into force about sixty years ago. It was a local Church law, confined to Elphin Diocese, to Roscommon County at least. A young woman had to be a sister or first cousin of deceased, a niece or daughter, before she could attend a wake at night.[68]

The folklore material shows that up to the beginning of the twentieth century young women did attend wakes in large numbers in all parts of Roscommon. In the areas of the county that were in the Elphin Diocese numbers dropped when it became a reserved sin (requiring absolution from the Bishop) for young women to attend. In Ballygar, County Galway, 'there were always big crowds at wakes, of men and women. There was no prohibition on women's attending a wake at night, as in some parts of Roscommon'.[69]

This liminal period, between death and burial, was always looked upon as a danger zone and people took different measures to protect themselves. 'People used to bring holy water in their pockets to sprinkle it, when they were going to wakes long ago. If they met anything they were frightened of, they had the holy water to sprinkle'.[70] In northeast Galway salt was used as a protection against supernatural forces. 'People going home from a wake used to put a grain of salt in their pockets as a precaution against spirits'.[71] Strength in numbers was the keynote at this transitional period, as the late Kevin Danaher of the Folklore Department at University College Dublin, pointed out: 'When going to or coming from a wake one should not be alone; at least two went together, and it was better still if people went in groups'.[72] This was a widely held belief; on the Cavan-Leitrim border, in the late 1950s, it was recorded: 'You should never leave a wake "your lone". This custom is still observed, never to leave a wake at night on your own'.[73] Fear of the spirits of the dead and of other supernatural forces made people wary. In the folklore accounts people who did not take proper precautions usually regretted their negligence.

The first thing that people did when they arrived at the corpse house was to go to where the body was laid out. They knelt down, said a prayer for the deceased and sprinkled the body with holy water. They then sympathized with the relatives on their loss. 'The usual form of sympathy is still the same as it always was: "I'm sorry for your trouble", and the answer is, "I know that"'.[74] In all areas the same form of sympathizing has been recorded and it has continued in use.

A custom recorded in north Offaly, which seems unique to one particular area, was:

> There used to be people called Purgatorians at wakes long ago, in the Kilcormac district. And they used to recite psalms or some kind of office at the wake. Then the following Sunday night, after the funeral, the Purgatorians would go back to the house where the death had occurred, and go over the same thing (i.e. recite the same office as they did at the wake).[75]

A Purgatorial society had been established, in the Diocese of Clonfert, in the mid nineteenth century to put an end to wake-abuses.[76] According to John Purcell of Kilcormac, County Offaly, the Purgatorians 'were nearly all from one townland, a townland called Coolfin. There were ten or twelve Purgatorians, who used to attend the wakes and they were all men'.[77] William Talbot recalled seeing them and explained their presence in that one district.

> A teacher from Skibbereen was teachin' here in Kilcormac – Henry Granger was his name – and he re-organised the Purgatorians. I heard them at wakes and I seen them in the chapel with a corpse. They all got around the coffin and sang an office. There were twelve or fourteen of them in it. They never took anything at a wake or corp' house. Granger made the arrangements that, as soon as the ceremony was over, they were all to lave the house.[78]

In Roscommon the Carmelites attended wakes:

The Carmelites were laymen, but they followed some religious rule, and they had a special burial plot in the churchyard of Kilteevan, with an iron railin's round it. They used to come to wakes and they'd sing hymns all night.[79]

There wasn't a lot thought of the Carmelites according to John Naughton, the former narrator. James Delaney said:

Any references I have ever heard to these 'Carmelites' – and they were very common in Longford – has almost without exception been derogatory. It seems to have been some kind of Third Order, like that of the Franciscans, of which they were members.[80]

Mary Anne Hanley of Derraghmylan, near Rooskey, had an aunt and 'she was one of them aul' votcheens (voteen) was out long ago, an aul' Carmelite. They used to go to the Chapel in Strokestown and a bad lot they were'.[81] In the material studied there is no mention in the later accounts, dealing with twentieth century traditions, of the Carmelites attending wakes.

Christiansen's description of wake tradition in Eastern Prussia is very similar to accounts in the folklore material in the midlands. 'Friends and neighbours filled the room, the men sitting on one side, and the women on the other. Hymns were sung, and spirits passed round, each in turn having his share'.[82] Large numbers of people attended the wake and chairs, stools and forms were often borrowed. 'There used to be big crowds at a wake in aul' times. And they used to get forms from the school and chairs from the neighbours'.[83] Most of the accounts are similar in describing how people were accommodated:

Usually long forms were placed along each wall of the kitchen for the people to sit on. If there were not sufficient forms, then a few long planks were procured and these were placed on stones, along the wall. If a man couldn't find a seat he would sit on another man's knee.

In the part of Roscommon referred to above (i.e. Parish of Cam), there was no distinction or segregation of the sexes, according to James Delaney. Men and women sat in the kitchen and women attended wakes as well as men.[84] Usually where the corpse was laid out determined where the people sat:

The women would be sitting around the table, and they'd sit faced out towards the kitchen, with their backs to the corpse. The custom then of waking the corpse on the table fell into disuse and the corpse was then left out on a bed in the bedroom. This room that the corpse was in was generally reserved for the women.[85]

Snuff and Clay Pipes

As soon as those who had gone for the requisites for the wake returned, neighbours gathered and helped with preparations. The first thing that was done was 'some one of them would take the snuff and put it on a plate and put the plate of snuff on the breast of the corpse'.[86] The use of snuff is widely attested in the folklore accounts, and it continued to be provided even when tobacco and tea became scarce during the war years.

> Tobacco, and its use in any of its forms, became known in Ireland only in the course of the seventeenth century so that its universal incorporation into the wake is a remarkable adaptation of new knowledge and new material into the functioning of an existing ritual.[87]

It was customary for people to take a pinch of snuff when they had said a prayer for the deceased. 'There were a couple of ounces of snuff left on the breast of the corpse, on a saucer, or a small plate and everyone that went up to the corpse took a pinch of snuff and said, "Lord have mercy on him" (or her)'.[88] In some areas the older women came specially prepared because they were fond of snuff. James Maxwell of Cootehall, north Roscommon, described the plate of snuff being left on the kitchen table and said it would be passed round to some of the women. 'And she'd be told to fill her canister'. (i.e. her snuff box, which was usually a Colman's mustard tin box, oval in shape, which held about an ounce or so).[89] The folklore accounts studied show that snuff continued in use into the first half of the twentieth century in some areas.

> Pipes and tobacco are gone out at wakes for more than forty years, but snuff is used yet. They put the snuff on a saucer and there'd be a row of people sittin' around in the corpse house, and the snuff would be handed around to them and everyone would take a pinch. It is the same then at the wake at night.[90]

It was recorded in west Longford in the late 1950s 'the snuff was always in the corpse room, and is still. There is always a little table beside the bed on which the corpse is laid out and the snuff is put on this table on a plate'.[91] In north Offaly 'snuff was handed round on a saucer during the wake and it was left on the table, on which the candles were, when not being handed round'.[92] Another account from the same area describes it as being left on the corpse's chest:

> The snuff was left on the corpse's chest all the time of the wake. Some aul' one would take the saucer o' snuff and hand it around, every now and then. We have a sayin' in this part of the country; "it went around like snuff at a wake".[93]

In the midlands most of the folklore accounts describe the snuff being placed on the corpse. It seems to have been customary to have the snuff as close to the corpse as possible and, like the candles, snuff had curative properties. It was believed in Longford that 'snuff left after the wake should be kept, as it cures a headache'.[94] The use of snuff is widely attested in the folklore accounts and it was still part of the ritual of death in the middle of the twentieth century in the midlands. 'A saucer of snuff is still put on the corpse. The saucer is placed on the legs of the corpse, just above the insteps'.[95]

Clay Pipes

> Taking nicotine – in the form of pipe-tobacco, tobacco snuff or cigarettes – is a primary duty of those assembled to wake the laid-out corpse and a male neighbour or neighbours of the deceased play the role of tobacco-priest, as it were, in the sacred location of the wake house, administering nicotine in one of its forms to all who are present.[96]

Although tobacco was not introduced to Ireland until the seventeenth century, its importance at the wake is strong in folklore belief which traces the origin of pipes and tobacco at wakes to the death of Jesus. In the Parish of Tobberclare, County Westmeath, the following was recorded: 'Wasn't Our Lord Himself waked. Didn't the Twelve Apostles wake him? They did. And that's when the pipes and tobacco were first used at any wake'.[97] In east Mayo, in the Parish of Kilmovee, the origin of pipes and tobacco was traced to Saint Thomas:

Ní raibh Naomh Tomás ag adhlacadh ár Shlánuightheoir.
Ní raibh sé sa mbaile, ach nuair a mhothaigh sé ar bhás ár
Shlánuightheoir chuaidh sé ar chuairt ag an uaigh. Shuidh
sé ar an leach a bhí os a chionn. Bhí an oiread sin brón air
faoi bhás ár Shlanuightheoir gur thoisigh sé ag piocadh an
caonach a bhí ag fás ar a leach. Chuir sé isteach i bpíopa é
agus thoisigh sé dhá chaitheamh. De bharr sin tá an tobach
beannuighthe agus bíonn píopaí agus tobac ag cuile
torraimh agus sochraidh ón lá sin go dtí an lá indiú.

[Saint Tomas wasn't at the burial of Our Saviour. He wasn't
at home but when he heard about Our Saviour he visited
the grave. He sat on the gravestone that was over him. He
was that sad about the death of Our Saviour that he began
to pluck the moss that was growing on the slab. He put it
into a pipe and he began to smoke it. Because of that
tobacco is blessed and you have pipes and tobacco at every
wake and every burial from that day to this].[98]

The old versions of the origin of pipes and tobacco at the
wake ascribe the origin to Our Lord, according to
Delaney, but he recorded a modern version in 1960, in
east Galway, about a soldier who came home to the
district from the West Indies.

Th' aul' men used to gather into his house after nightfall to
hear the wonders the soldier seen out abroad. And this aul'
soldier made the rule to fill the pipe and give everyone a
smoke when they'd come in. He had plenty of tobacco
always. Then he left it by will that there'd be tobacco and
pipes at his wake, in memory of all the nights they used to
be smoking around the fire. So the neighbours all thought it
was a good idea and ever after that there was pipes and
tobacco at wakes.[99]

The custom of having clay pipes at wakes and funerals is
widely attested, and large quantities of pipes were
provided filled with tobacco. The clay pipes used at
wakes were cheap and generally a gross or more were
bought with the tobacco. 'For my mother's wake in 1905
(says John Flanagan) there was ten pounds of tobacco at
four shillings a pound, and there was four or five gross
of pipes'.[100] In the material studied it was generally a
gross of pipes that was usually bought for the wake
although in some accounts it was more. In Athleague it
was recorded that a few gross of pipes were bought:

Three or four gross of pipes would be bought and if there
were any left over they'd be brought back to the shop, but
indeed very few were ever left over because they'd break
them and be peggin' them at one another.[101]

Most of the narrators refer to young men breaking off the shanks of the pipes to use as missiles and in some instances people were injured. According to John Gately of Coolagarry, County Roscommon, 'many a young fellow learned to smoke at a wake. They used to get as many pipes as they could and break the shanks off them, and put the heads full of tobacco in their pockets'.[102] In the midlands it was usually the pipes made in Knockcroghery village that were used and they were nearly always described as having long shanks.

> A wake pipe was known as 'a Lord have mercy' (because everyone said on accepting a pipe, "Lord have mercy on him/her"). They were made specially for wakes and no one smoked them except at wakes. They were made in the clay pipe factory at Knockcroghery. These pipes had very long shanks on them, a foot or so long, and on the head of the pipe was the letter 'L'.[103]

The production of clay pipes in Knockcroghery can be traced to the early nineteenth century. Isaac Weld visited the village in 1832 and described the manufacture of the pipes and their appearance:

> The pipes are of the most humble description, short in the stem and small in the bole; yet in quality, the ware seems to be as tough and as white as that of the pipes of superior size and workmanship from other countries. In the larger towns even of the county of Roscommon, they are held in low estimation; their chief consumption is for wakes, where the low price, and the small quantity of tobacco required to fill them, insure them a preference.[104]

In the folklore collected by James Delaney, from the 1950s through to the 1970s, William Curley was named as owner of the factory in Knockcroghery. 'Curley had a boy and this boy used to go around the country sellin' the pipes. One week he'd go Strokestown direction and another week in Ballygar direction. Another week he'd be off in Longford'.[105] An old man in Longford told James Delaney that the boy travelled into Cavan and Westmeath also.

Kieran Mc Manus of Nure, south Roscommon, who was 88 years of age in 1962, said the first pipes he saw at wakes 'had a short shank and a bit of a knob on the end of the bowl'.[106] The older men preferred the pipes with a short shank as they were pleasant to smoke. Most of the folklore accounts describe the pipes as having long shanks and these were only used for wakes. However there are some references to the "Forty-three" which was the most popular pipe made in Knockcroghery. 'There was a very good pipe out about forty years ago or more. It was called Forty-three. It had the figure "43," stamped on it. It was a good soft clay pipe'.[107] The manufacture of clay pipes continued in Knockcroghery until 1921, when most of the village was burned down by the Black and Tans.[108] Some of the folklore accounts trace the abandonment of pipes at wakes to this date.

Knockcroghery after the Black and Tans burning in 1919

A few men were in charge of filling the pipes for the wake as it was customary for everyone who visited the wake house to be offered a pipe whether they smoked or not:

> The tobacco was cheap twist tobacco and was known as "corp' house tobacco". The pipes were put into a skib [wicker tray] or basket, and someone went about the house with the skib full of pipes and distributed them among the people.[109]

In the earlier accounts the narrators said it was always twist tobacco and it came in a big roll. The wake pipes had a small bowl so it didn't take much tobacco to fill them.

I remember the time you'd get no tobacco, only twist, and that was the kind you bought for wakes. They didn't 'bruise' the tobacco. They just cut a lump of tobacco and put it in the pipe. Then you'd have to cut it up fine yourself and 'bruise' it, and fill the pipe properly yourself.[110]

In Roscommon you could refuse a pipe if you were a non-smoker, unlike some other counties:

It wasn't like Longford, where everyone, men and women, were given pipes and they were expected to light the pipe, at least. A woman who was a non smoker, or a man, would put a match to the pipe and so fulfilled the obligation of smoking it.[111]

In northeast Galway: 'You would be offered a pipe, but it wasn't necessary to take it. You could take one if you liked. If you didn't, it excited no comment'.[112] What was important was that you said 'Lord have mercy on the dead', when the pipe was offered so that the deceased got the benefit of the prayer.

There are differences in the material investigated as to when the custom of having pipes and tobacco at wakes ended. In 1959, Mrs Ward of Athleague, said her father had died fifty-three years previously and 'that wake was the last one, in that neighbourhood, to have pipes and tobacco and snuff'.[113] Other accounts give later dates: the burning of the clay pipe factory in Knockcroghery in 1921 or the First or Second World Wars. According to Ellen Hogan, of Four Roads, 'the custom of having pipes and tobacco at wakes has gone out since the time of the First World War. Tobacco became scarce at that time and began to get dear, also, so the custom was discontinued'.[114] In South Roscommon it was recorded: 'There have been no pipes and tobacco at wakes in Clonown since the time the tobacco was scarce in the war years of the Second World War'.[115] Thomas Horan of Ballyduff, County Offaly, remembered clearly when the custom died out. 'My eldest son died twenty years ago (i.e. 1943) and I wanted to get pipes for the wake, but they told me that the pipes were done away with. So that's how I know how long the custom is gone out'.[116] Tobacco smoking was an important part of the ritual of the wake and when clay pipes disappeared cigarettes were substituted in their place. In the 1950s it was recorded in west Longford that 'pipes at wakes are going out of fashion, they do get a few clay pipes for old people, but not nearly what they bought forty years ago. Cigarettes now are more common at wakes'.[117]

Refreshments

> The kind of funeral feasting reported from the wake as practised in the non-elite popular culture of the late nineteenth and early twentieth century Ireland represents a ritual intensification of experience in the liminal domain of the laid-out corpse by means of the communal ingestion of tobacco and alcohol on the one hand and of festive forms of subsistence food on the other.[118]

People were conscious that everything possible should be done to ensure that there was plenty of food and drink at the wake, even if it meant putting themselves in debt. It was customary according to the early accounts to have whiskey at the corpse house and wake. Porter became popular in the 1920s when whiskey became more expensive. Women drank wine and minerals and everyone was served tea during the day and after midnight. The rite of eating and drinking together has been identified by van Gennep as 'a rite of incorporation, of physical union'.[119] It can be clearly seen from the folklore material how important it was that the deceased be given their due whatever the cost. Nobody was allowed leave the corpse house or wake without some form of refreshment.

According to the older narrators whiskey not porter, was served at the wake. Joseph Hanley of Kilteevan parish, who was 95 years of age in 1958, said, 'in my young days there was no drink only whiskey at wakes. There was no such thing as porter at a wake or a weddin', only whiskey. Porter came in later in half barrels, for wakes and funerals'.[120] In north Offaly whiskey was plentiful at wakes in the narrator's youth. 'In my time I never seen anything but whiskey at the wake or funeral. There used to be jars and jars of it'.[121] The prevalence of whiskey may have been due to the fact that there were many more distilleries in Ireland in the nineteenth century than currently and whiskey was relatively cheap. The whiskey was of poor quality, like the tobacco, and was known as "corp' house whiskey". The term "corp' house whiskey" was derogatory according to James Delaney, who referred to a bill for "burial charges", which he had been shown by a man named Donohoe, of Legga, County Longford. 'The date on the bill head was 1892, and the biggest item and the first one was eight gallons of whiskey @ 17/6 (i.e. seventeen shillings and six pence) a gallon'.[122] Later in the twentieth century, whiskey was replaced by porter for general consumption at the wake but whiskey was still provided for those involved in making the coffin and in laying out and burying the corpse.

> In 1914 they cut out the pipes and tobacco and began to bring in a half barrel of porter instead. The only people ever to get whiskey at a wake in the Mount Talbot area would be near relatives and the man that dug the grave and those who laid out the corpse.[123]

Some accounts were different, depending on peoples' circumstances. When Mary Anne Hanley's father died (c. 1911) the priest asked her not to have drink at the wake, as her father had signed a paper at the mission that there wouldn't be drink at a wake in his house, but she refused because she didn't want 'a mane wake'. The priest asked her to keep the drink upstairs, as they had a two storey house, so she compromised. 'We had no porter at all at the wake. Me father would never drink porter and wouldn't have it in the house. So we had two gallons of whiskey in this room upstairs'.[124] Thomas Lucas of Clonfert, east Galway, also referred to missioners banning drink at wakes. When one of his brothers died they got eleven and a half gallons of whiskey for the wake the first night and he had to go to Shannonbridge the next day for two and a half gallons more. 'Well that was in 1904 and there was a mission the same year and the missioners put a stop to drink at the wakes. Another brother o' mine died the next year and there was no drink at that wake'.[125]

Thomas Lucas

Relatives and neighbours were in charge of serving the alcohol during the wake. 'Usually the barrel of porter would be in a shed or outhouse, where it would be tapped and the men in charge of giving it out would bring the porter in buckets, and then give it to the men in mugs'.[126] Men were offered a drink of porter as soon as they sat down and more was served throughout the night.

Customs began to change as the twentieth century progressed and fewer instances of drunkenness were recorded than in earlier times. In Mountplunket it was recorded: 'A lot of people at the wake would get a couple of pints of porter, but they wouldn't get enough to make them drunk'.[127] An account from Swanlinbar, County Cavan, is similar: 'Not so long ago they used to get a quarter barrel or half barrel of porter or stout.

Nowadays no one gets a quarter barrel, but they get three or four cases of stout now'.[128]

In all of the folklore accounts studied, the Rosary was said at twelve midnight and tea was given to everyone afterwards, as part of the ritual of the wake.

> The Rosary is always said at midnight, and it was the custom ever. Someone that would be a good warrant to give it out, would give out the Rosary. There was no difference between the Rosary said at the wake and that at any other time. The Litany of the Blessed Virgin was also said and instead of sayin' "pray for us" they'd say "pray for him," if it was a man was dead, or "pray for her," if it was a woman was dead.[129]

According to one of the narrators, 'tea would be going on nearly all the time of the wake, day and night. Neighbouring girls and women would be in charge of that. There would be rounds of porter in between, and wine for the women'.[130] Most of the folklore sources emphasized that tea was served after midnight, bread and butter was served with it and sometimes jam.

> There used to be tay at all the wakes, about one o'clock in the mornin'. Big four pound loaves would be bought for the wake always and a lot went to the wake for the loaves. The tay was given out in the room. During the day, at the corp' house, it wasn't so much tay would be given, but everyone that went to the corp' house was treated, porter, or whiskey or claret punch.[131]

Some of the folklore material referred to tea being given out again at daylight before people left the wake house. 'Them that would stay the night would get it secondly. They'd be sure to get tay before they'd lave the house, around daylight in the mornin'. Everyone took tay and no one was allowed not to'.[132] In most of the counties investigated, in the midlands, where the narrators were elderly and were referring to the end of the nineteenth and beginning of the twentieth century, it was the custom to have one meal. During the war years when tea and butter became scarce people were often served porter only with dry bread. It depended on what the family could afford. Later when people became more affluent, other refreshments were served and a variety of drinks. What was important was that the ritual of eating together was observed as it was an essential rite of incorporation.

Games

Seán Ó Súilleabháin and Henry Morris believed that the origin of playing games at wakes could be traced to the Cluichthe Caointe, or Games of Lamentation, which took place when a great warrior died in Ireland.[133] The same belief is reflected in folklore from Athleague: 'When the King died in Tara, they'd spend a fortnight playing games and dancing, and that's how the games started to be played at wakes and they went on from generation to generation up to about sixty years ago'.[134] Wood–Martin believed the plays and games had a pagan origin: 'At wakes there were in use plays, games and sports which appear to have been essentially of pagan origin, and of such a character that although at first tolerated, yet in more civilized days they were suppressed'.[135] Most of the material investigated shows that the games continued up to the first decade of the twentieth century and in some instances even longer. They were part of the tradition of the wake and were accepted as such. 'The wake games were played at all wakes up to about fifty years ago. The clergy did not object to them and the people of the house in which the wake was held didn't object either'.[136]

Until nightfall the corpse house was quiet and sombre and the time was spent in recalling old memories and chatting generally about local issues. From nine or ten o'clock on as the young people began to arrive the whole atmosphere changed and became charged with energy. Connolly, historian, suggests that:

> The celebrations of the festive wake derived part of their vigour from the fact that they were an assertion of continued vitality in the face of a sudden reminder of universal mortality, and of continuity in the face of the abrupt removal from a close-knit community of one of its members.[137]

Games which were tests of agility and strength have been recorded throughout the country. Some of the games were described by William Carlton in the form of a short story, 'Larry Mc Farlan's Wake', set at the beginning of the nineteenth century, in County Tyrone. Lady Wilde, in the last decades of the nineteenth century, wrote that 'wake ceremonies are still held in the Irish cabins, where the men drink and smoke, and tell ancient stories; though the highly dramatic games of former times have almost entirely died out'.[138] Henry Morris got an account of the games played in County Monaghan from his uncle and they represent what was current from about 1870 to 1900.[139] Carlton who attended wakes and played these games described a slapping game called Hot-Loof which was usually the first game played and said, 'you might as well get a stroke of a sledge as a blow from some of them able, hard-working fellows, with hands upon them like lime stone'.[140] The same game was described as a slapping game in Galway. In the midlands games similar to those described by Carlton, Morris and Wilde, have been recorded:

> To start the fun a man would stand up in the middle of the floor and then stoop down, from the hips, as if making a back for leap-frog. Then he put one hand on his back with the palm upwards, and the back of the hand resting on his back. Another man came then and gave the stooping man two leadógs (i.e. smacks) on the upturned hand, with his open hand. Then a second man took the same position and so on.[141]

According to Delaney the game that was most popular of all the wake games he collected was 'Fox Harra'. In Roscommon it was called "Fox Harra" or Thart; in Longford and Westmeath "Harra Harra" and in Wexford "Hunt the Slipper" or "Hurry the Brogue".

> The players sit in a circle with their knees up and passed an instrument such as an old boot or shoe, straw rope or knotted hemp rope from one to the other under their legs. While the player standing in middle of the circle went searching under their legs to try and find it he got many a smack as he had his back to the man in possession of the rope or whatever it was. The game was also known as "The Fool in the Middle".[142]

Generally the people of the house did not take part in the games but according to Michael Gilligan of Cornageer, County Roscommon, two brothers, 'Tom Gately and Bernie had the "fox herra" made for their father's wake, the night he died. In this area the game gets its name from the instrument used to play it. This was a short thick rope made of the bark of a tree'.[143]

In northeast Galway, according to Martin Nolan of Lissavruggy:

> The games were played at every wake where an old person died. They wouldn't have any games at a young person's

wake. At a young person's wake they might sing a song, but they went on with no boisterous behaviour, such as the games entailed. People did not object to the games being played at a wake, but if they object did no games would be played.[144]

Slapping games were popular at wakes in the midlands but those described were more endurance tests than games. 'You'd go out to the middle of the floor and put out your hand for three blows. Some of them fellows had hands like steel and one of them would come along and see could you stand three blows from him'.[145] Henry Morris referred to a master of ceremonies taking charge of the games; 'in Connacht he was called the Cleasaidhe, he was one of the country boys of a masterful disposition, whose nomination was generally assented to'.[146] Patrick Reilly of Granard, County Longford, who was usually Master of Ceremonies at wake games, described for James Delaney the special preparations he made. 'He would get an old shank of a clay pipe and heat it in the fire, and then rub the hot shank between the palms of his two hands. In that way he'd burn the skin of his palms and put a thick coating on them'. Usually women did not take part in the games but in the Granard area, according to the narrator, 'women also particularly the middle aged women took part in the games and some of them could "shuffle the brogue" as well as any man'.[147] Games were played all over County Longford, according to Margaret Rogers of Aughintemple.

They ceased about thirty years ago when the wakes were confined to one night and the body taken to the chapel for the rest of the time before burial. Usually men only took part in the wake games and these games did not take place till after midnight. Then they usually went on all night. Women, as a rule did not attend at night.[148]

In Kilteevan, east Roscommon, the following games were played: Riding the Grey Mare, Scollop the Turkey, Cíoradh an Chait, Travelling the Tongs, Thady told me, The Crooked Crabtree and The Wee Polony Man.[149] Scollop the Turkey was similar to a game in Wexford called 'The Cockfight' according to Delaney and women played it too. It involved two players who were trussed so that movement was practically impossible. A scallop was put in each player's hands and they had to try to prod each other with the scallop. Whoever succeeded in knocking over the other playor was the victor.

> The old man who told me about it said that a woman down the road was the best at it and could beat all the men. Whether it was only this particular game they played or not I don't know, but as a rule the women did not take part in the games, except the "Marrying Game", of course.[150]

The game Cíoradh an Chait is very similar to the games 'Hold the Light' and 'Wink' recorded in other areas. A fellow was picked out and he had to cross his arms across his body and cover his ears with his hands; his hands were turned palm outwards. A second player got a candle and held it before his eyes so that he was blinded. The other players took turns striking his hands and the unfortunate man was supposed to guess who struck him. Other games recorded in the midlands include The Beehive, The Mulberry Tree, Cooling the Still or Drowning the Still, Fair Judge and Foul Judge, Hunt the Buck and The Tailor. The description of the game The Tailor which James Delaney got from Michael Gilligan, aged 92, was he said the best description ever he got of the game.

> The game was a representation of the tailor's shop, with as many working men, journey men tailors, all working under the direction of a master tailor. All the journeymen, five or six players, sat around in a ring, on the floor, while the master looked on to see the work was properly done. The customer for whom the suit was being made was also present, looking on. Each journeyman had a different part of the suit to make. They sang as they worked, and the master tailor was armed with a big belt and went about walloping the workmen for idling. When the suit would be finished, the customer would be asked for the money and he wouldn't have it. Then in the words of Michael Gilligan, "they'd put that man up on their arms, and flog the brains out of him".[151]

The game The Tailor was known in Leitrim and Longford as Sewing the Coat. Jack Duignan of Gortlettera, south Leitrim, who was about twelve years when he saw this game played, described it to a neighbour.

They all sat round in a ring and used real needles and thread to sew the coat and sang songs while they were doing it. Then they jumped to their feet and began b'atin each other through the house with the aul' coat. Then some of them put a pipe in the corps' mouth. The corpse got shook several times when they were playin' the tricks.[152]

Sometimes the games degenerated into sheer horseplay as in the case of the former which bears little resemblance to Sewing the Big Coat as described in other material or by Ó Súilleabháin.[153] It depended on who was in charge and whether they could control the young men, or whose house the games were being played in. According to Patrick Mac Donnell of Caltra, County Roscommon, who had been a participant in some of the games, 'there was no regularity or Christianity. In some houses they would be far rowdier and uncontrolled than in others. In a poor person's house they went to the devil altogether'.[154] John Naughton, of Kilteevan, remembered Thart, Enlisting for a Soldier and Feedy Fawdry is my Name, being played; the latter was a memorizing game. 'There was a captain over the game, who called himself Feedy Fawdry. He gave names to all the players, and each player had to remember every other player's name'. The penalty for not answering correctly was a saucepan of cold water down your sleeve.[155] Feedy Fawdry is the same type of game as My Man Jack, which is also known as Cock in the Corner or Priest of the Parish in east Roscommon. In the Boyle area, where the game was known as My Man Jack, it began with the following rhyme: 'The priest o' the parish has lost his considerin' cap some say this and some say that and some say, my man Jack'.[156]

In north-west Roscommon, in material gathered in 1938, it was felt that the games were used as an excuse for avenging old scores. One of the games played was Old Hen, in which the leader was armed with a reaping hook and 'he had the privilege of striking anybody whom he had a grudge against while calling "chuck, chuck." Bróg about was played differently, but the same motive was attached to the game vis. of avenging a grudge against a neighbour'. Ratha was another game which was similar to Bróg but a rope was used in it. The Nine Daughters was a favourite game, among the people who lived in the Geevagh district (County Sligo), according to the narrator.[157] The Nine Daughters was popular in Longford also. 'It was a match making game a simplified variant of 'Old Dowd and his daughters', according to Delaney.[158]

The clergy condemned the mock marriages performed at wakes and some suggested they were as binding as marriages performed in church. As young women were prohibited from attending wakes in Elphin Diocese from the beginning of the twentieth century this may account for the marrying game not being played in many areas of Roscommon. James Delaney said he had often heard from old people that "there used to be marryin' at wakes" but John Gately, senior, was the only person he met who had actually witnessed the game. He saw it performed in Taughmaconnell which was not part of Elphin Diocese.

> The marriage ceremony was gone through, just as it was done before the priest. Some man did the priest and he called up a boy and girl to marry them, using the same words as the priest uses. When the marriage was over, the groom would be told to kiss the bride and that's where the fun began. Other fellows would want to kiss the bride as well.[159]

The elaborate plays and mimes described by Lady Wilde and Wood-Martin in the nineteenth century were not recorded in folklore investigated in the midlands. Some of the games referred to were actually played in rambling houses and that is where the informants saw them. 'These games were not only played at wakes but at all rambling houses (where neighbours gathered to talk and tell stories) at night time'.[160]

Games at wakes continued to be played later in the twentieth century in Galway and Mayo according to the folklore accounts. In material recorded from the early 1960s in east Galway: 'The villages of Kilmore and Tully were noted in former times for the best men at slapping at wakes. "He was a great slapper in his time." You'd hear that said about an aul' man even yet. About twenty years ago the slapping at wakes stopped'.[161] Mrs Ward said in her memory 'no games were ever played at the Roscommon wakes, but only in Galway'. She remembered games being played at her grandmother's wake, in Ballygar.[162] In east Mayo, the following games were played in one Philip Waldron's youth: Crúiscín, Fromsa Framsa, Bosuigheacht, An Liathróid, An Crios, An Naipcín, My Man Jack and An Gabhar. As Morris points out:

> The change of language must have meant a great change in the wake games, as any game with set words or speeches – and these constituted the majority – had to be radically modified, or a new set of words composed in English to suit the game.[163]

In Roscommon and Offaly the younger narrators do not associate games with wakes but remember riddles, story telling, singing and barging. 'The people passed their time at the wake in talk and chat, and telling yarns. One fellow would tell a yarn and someone else would try to better it. There were no wake games'.[164]

Singing

Singing was a popular pastime at wakes in the midlands and people travelled distances to hear and to take part in the competitions. 'Singing was a regular feature of all wakes. Every man able to sing had to sing at the wake. It didn't matter whether the dead person was young or old, there was still singing'.[165] The latter reference is unusual because in most of the material investigated it appears to have been customary to have singing only at the wake of an older person. At a younger person's wake there was no singing unless the people of the house gave permission. 'The singing occurred only at wakes of old people, where there would not be much grief. One singer was called on one side of the house, then another on the other side'.[166] On the Sligo-Leitrim border it was recorded: 'When I was a wee lad I heard them singing at them (i.e. wakes). No, I never heard of them playing games'.[167] Singing of hymns by the Carmelites and The Purgatorians at wakes in the midlands has already been referred to, but in earlier accounts the songs were not religious. In northwest Roscommon the songs that featured at wakes were generally Nationalist ones. 'Old men seem to like Fenian songs better than any other, especially if they are asked to sing at a wake. "The Peeler and the Goat" was sometimes a favourite with old men'.[168] On the Offaly-Westmeath border it was recorded: 'I used to hear tell of them travellin' across the country to a wake and there'd be a competition of songs all night, one singin' again th' other'.[169]

Barging

Barging was common at wakes in the midlands until the beginning of the twentieth century, but it seems to have died out earlier than the other traditional wake pastimes. It was known by different terms: in north Roscommon it was called 'Scalding' and in the south of the county 'Heckling' but the most common term was 'Barging'. James Delaney explains it thus:

> Barging in local speech means a competition in repartee. Two men who would be well known for their quickness of wit and speech would begin making personal remarks to each other. The barging went on till one or other gave up. It was also common practice at wakes in Longford.[170]

The barging was for the benefit of the audience and it was usually very personal. John Kenny could remember barging matches in south Roscommon: 'Two fellows would be barging one another, and telling stories, one trying to get the better of the other'.[171] Some had a reputation as barges and their performance was looked forward to by those assembled for the wake. Thomas Kelly from Taughmaconnell could remember barging at wakes:

> George Galvin of Cloonlaughlin and Mike Mc Donnell of Jamestown were famous for bargin' at wakes. They'd never sit near one another but sat in the far corners of the kitchen and then they'd begin to barge one another across the kitchen.[172]

In the North of Ireland the term used for barging was 'mobbing' and it followed the same form as that described in material collected in the midlands. It started between two from different localities and as it proceeded others joined in until in the end you might have one parish against another. 'Both sides, aimed at making it humorous, for the side that provoked the greatest laughter was regarded as the successful one'.[173] It was referred to as 'mobbing' also in north Longford where it was common practice at wakes, and 'there were fellows who were famous for it'.[174] In north Offaly the narrator, who was born in 1898, knew about barging but said 'I didn't see much of that in my time only very little. 'Twas dead out in my time'.[175]

End of the Wakes

'By the beginning of the nineteenth century, the practices of the festive wake had long been an object of ecclesiastical condemnation and prohibition'.[176] As a result of the opposition of the church, the form of the wakes began to change so that the scenes of drunkenness and games which were of a sexual nature and parodied religion were no longer being enacted at the end of the nineteenth century.

> A national synod of bishops, meeting at Maynooth in 1875, declared: 'Parish priests must put an end to unchristian wakes, where the corpse is present and where games, dances, singing and drinking are carried on – these abuses are a shame and a disgrace to the house of the dead'. A similar prohibition was repeated by the national synod of 1927.[177]

From this period, the late 1920s, the wake was reduced to one night and the corpse was brought to the church the night before the burial. James Delaney recorded in Kiltoom that before it became obligatory to bring the corpse to the Church for one night, people who lived close to the church, 'they'd put the corpse for a night in the church'. Delaney pointed out 'this is the first time I ever heard of this being done, before the practice became obligatory on all'.[178] According to John Stroker, 'in 1905, the first curate came to Kilteevan and that finished the wakes. They had to bring the corpse to the chapel, then, so the wakes stopped'.[179] Delaney feels the narrator was incorrect as the date was too early; in most of the folklore accounts the two nights wake continued to the 1920s. An early date was recorded also in north Offaly: 'I remember the first man they brought to the chapel. He was a man named Andy Lightnin. It was about 1905'.[180]

Morris referring to barn wakes points out that 'the absence of the corpse was the cause of the decay of the old fashioned wake'.[181] Wake practices had altered by the end of the nineteenth century in Ireland and Continental Europe and continued to change throughout the twentieth century, not alone because of regulations instituted by the Church, but because of outside influences. In 1959, it was recorded in Roscommon 'the wakes are now almost a thing of the past. The Parish Priest of Mount Talbot wants every corpse to go to the Church, if the person dies before ten in the morning'.[182] In north Offaly wakes seem to have died out at about the same time.

> When the custom came in to bring the corpse for one night to the chapel, people said it wasn't natural for the corpse to be l'avin' its own house for the Chapel. They got used to it then and nowadays they don't keep the corpse in the house at all, even for one night.[183]

But some areas like Kiltoom in south Roscommon held on to the old traditions later, according to James Delaney. 'Today, as I write (4th June '74) my neighbour, an old man of about seventy six, lies dead in his house. He died at 4.30. p.m. yesterday and there was a wake'.[184]

Ariès has pointed out that in the course of the twentieth century death changed, and an absolutely new type of dying made its appearance, 'the invisible death'.

> The dying man's bedroom has passed from the home to the hospital. For technical medical reasons, this transfer has been accepted by families, and popularized and facilitated by their complicity. The hospital has become the place of the solitary death.[185]

Society in Ireland changed radically from the 1960s onwards, wakes went out of fashion, as outside agencies influenced our treatment of death. Funeral homes of the American type have taken the place of the corpse house since the 1970s.

Notes

1   Anon. *Dublin University Magazine*, 88, 1876, 292-96; 295.
2   S. Ó Súilleabháin, *Irish Wake Amusements*, Cork 1997, 23.
3   IFC1480:181, collected by James Delaney from James Dolan, Kiltycreeva, Ballinamuck, Co. Longford, 1957.
4   Patricia Lysaght, 'Caoineadh ós Cionn Coirp: The Lament for the Dead in Ireland', *Folklore* 108 (1997), 65-82; 69.
5   IFC 1771:19-21, collected by James Delaney from James Flynn, Shurock, Co. Westmeath, July 1967.
6   IFC 1677:286.
7   IFC 1736:218, collected by James Delaney from William Rourke, Cloonkeen, Castlerea, Co. Roscommon, Nov. 1966.

[8] IFC 552:306, collected by Kathleen Hurley at Ballymoe, Co. Galway, 1938.

[9] IFC 1550:209, collected by James Delaney from John Noone, Kilclough, Toomard, Ballinasloe, Co. Galway, Sept. 1959.

[10] IFC 1506:537-538, collected by James Delaney from Mrs Kate Ward, Corra More, Athleague, Co. Roscommon, June 1959.

[11] IFC 1639:168.

[12] IFC 1575:501, collected by James Delaney from Kieran Mc Manus, Nure, Co. Roscommon, Feb. 1962.

[13] Interview, April 2003.

[14] IFC 1639:167, collected by James Delaney from John Ledwidth, America, Moor, Co. Roscommon, Oct. 1962.

[15] IFC 1639:237, collected by James Delaney from John Kenny, Newtown, Kiltoom, Co. Roscommon, 1962.

[16] IFC 1487:74, collected by James Delaney from James Farrell, Furze, Lagan, Co. Longford, Oct. 1957.

[17] 1676:34-35, collected by James Delaney from John Purcell, Money, Kilcormac, Co. Offaly, Sept. 1963.

[18] IFC 1677:286, collected by James Delaney from Thomas Daly, Cloonyderg, Co. Offaly, Sept. 1963.

[19] IFC 1526:156, collected by James Delaney from Charles Furey, Mountplunket, Co. Roscommon, Feb. 1959.

[20] IFC 549:341, collected by Bríd Ní Ghamhnáin at Ballindoon, Boyle, Co. Roscommon, 1938.

[21] IFC 1507:169, collected by James Delaney from Patrick Mc Govern, Swanlinbar, Co. Cavan, 1959.

[22] P. Ariès, *At the Hour of Our Death*, 169.

[23] Ibid., 206.

[24] B.S. Puckle, *Funeral Customs: Their Origin and Development*, Detroit 1990, 37.

[25] S. Ó Cinnéide, 'Foclóireacht "Faoi Chlár" agus "Tórramh"', *Feasta* Lúnasa 1980, 19.

[26] IFC 1526:46, collected by James Delaney from James Grady, Rinnegan, St. John's, Co. Roscommon, Dec. 1959.

[27] IFC 1677:329, collected by James Delaney from William Talbot, Kilcormac, Co Offaly, 1963.

[28] IFC 1782:23, collected by Michael Murphy from John Currid, Sooey, Co. Sligo, 1970.

[29] A Gailey, 'A Wicker Coffin from Ballysheil Graveyard, Annaclone, County Down', *Ulster Folklife* 17 (1971), 89-90.

[30] IFC 1506:144, collected by James Delaney from John Naughton, Aughmagree, Kilteevan, Co. Roscommon, Feb. 1958.

[31] IFC 1551:385, collected by James Delaney from John Gately (Senior), Coolagarry, Castletown, Co Roscommon, Feb. 1960.

[32] IFC 1487:72, collected by James Delaney from James Farrell, Furze, Lagan, Co. Longford, Oct. 1957.

[33] IFC 1487:407, collected by James Delaney from Eugene Clarke and James Nolan, Ohill, Co Longford, Dec. 1957.

[34] IFC 1639:168, collected by James Delaney from John Ledwidth, America, Moor, Co. Roscommon, Sept. 1962.

[35] IFC 1550:289, collected by James Delaney from Michael Coughlan, Closhatoher, Co. Galway, Sept. 1958.

[36] Ibid., 288-9.

[37] IFC 1487:73, collected by James Delaney from James Farrell, Furze, Lagan, Co. Longford, Oct. 1957

[38] IFC 549:35, collected by Bríd Ní Ghamhnáin, at Ballindoon, Co Roscommon, 1938.

[39] IFC 1551:158, collected by James Delaney from James Nolan, Mount Talbot, Co. Roscommon, Dec. 1959.

[40] IFC 1771:26, collected by James Delaney from James Flynn, Shurock, Co. Westmeath, July 1967.

[41] IFC 1781:243-245, collected by James Delaney from William Maxwell, Dorrary, Boyle Co. Roscommon, 1970.

[42] IFC 1550:289-90, collected by James Delaney from Michael Coughlan, Closhatoher, Co. Galway, Sept. 1958.

[43] IFC 1487:73, collected by James Delaney from James Farrell, Furze, Lagan, Co. Longford, Oct. 1957.

[44] IFC 1550:289, collected by James Delaney from Michael Coughlan, Closhatoher, Co. Galway, Sept. 1958, 289.

[45] Information received from Thomas Shaughnessy, Rahara Co. Roscommon, August 2003.

[46] IFC 552:309, collected by Kathleen Hurley at, Ballymoe, Co. Galway, 1938.

[47] IFC 1839:57, collected by James Delaney from William Rourke, Cloonkeen, Castlerea, Co. Roscommon, 1973.

[48] P. Healy, *God Save All Here: Memories of Life in Co. Roscommon in the 20th Century*, Roscommon 1999, 89.

[49] Lysaght, 'Caoineadh os Cionn Coirp: The Lament for the Dead in Ireland', 74.

[50] S. Ó Catháin, 'Caointeoireacht an Chine Daonna', B. Ó Madagáin eag., in *Gnéithe Den Chaointeoireacht*, Baile Átha Cliath 1978, 9-19; 12-3.

[51] IFC 549:320, collected by Bríd Ní Ghamhnáin at Ballindoon, Boyle, Co. Roscommon, 1938.

[52] IFC 1677:347, collected by James Delaney from John Connaughton, Lisduff, Co. Offaly, Sept. 1963.

[53] IFC 1575:28, collected by James Delaney from Michael Moore, Kilkenny, Co. Roscommon, Autumn 1961.

[54] IFC 1677:362, collected by James Delaney from Thomas Horan, Ballyduff,, Co. Offaly, June, 1964.

[55] IFC 1639:270.

[56] Edward Egan, interview, April 2003.

[57] Lysaght, 'Caoineadh os Cionn Coirp: The Lament for the Dead in Ireland', 74.

[58] E. Muir, *Ritual in Early Modern Europe*, Cambridge 1997, 48.

[59] IFC 1550:167, collected by James Delaney from Patrick Mac Donnell, Caltra, Co. Roscommon, 1958.

[60] Christiansen, 'The Dead and The Living', 28.

[61] IFC 1551:157, collected by James Delaney from James Nolan, Mount Talbot, Co. Roscommon, Dec. 1959.

[62] IFC 1575:503, collected by James Delaney from Kieran Mac Manus, Nure, Co. Roscommon, Feb. 1962.

[63] IFC 1677:287, collected by James Delaney from Thomas Daly, Cloonyderg, Ballynahowan, Co. Offaly, Oct. 1963.

[64] IFC 1640:96, collected by James Delaney from John Quigley, Killinure Point, Glasson, Co. Westmeath, 1963.

[65] Ó Suilleabháin, Irish Wake Amusements, 172.

[66] Christiansen, 'The Dead and The Living', 27.

[67] IFC 1507:428, collected by James Delaney from James Grady, Rinnegan, St. John's, Co. Roscommon, Nov. 1958.

[68] IFC 1506:536, collected by James Delaney from Mrs. Kate Ward, Corra More, Athleague, Co. Roscommon, June 1958.

[69] IFC 1550:181, collected by James Delaney from Martin Nolan, Lissavruggy, Ballygar, Co. Galway, 1959.

[70] IFC 1639:262, collected by James Delaney from John Kenny, Newtown, Kiltoom, Co. Roscommon, 1963.

[71] IFC 1550:281, collected by James Delaney from Michael Coughlan, Closhatoher, Co. Galway, Sept. 1959.

[72] Danaher, In Ireland Long Ago, 144.

[73] IFC 1507:168, collected by James Delaney from Patrick Mc Govern, Swanlinbar, Co Cavan, 1958.

[74] IFC 1550:167, recorded by James Delaney from Patrick Mac Donnell, Caltra, Athlone, Co. Roscommon, 1959.

[75] IFC 1676:33-4, collected by James Delaney from John Purcell, Money, Kilcormac, Co. Offaly.

[76] Ó Súilleabháin, Irish Wake Amusements, 164.

[77] IFC 1676:4, collected by James Delaney from John Purcell, Money, Kilcormac, Co. Offaly..

[78] IFC 1677:119-20, collected by James Delaney from William Talbot, Kilcormac, Co. Offaly, 1964.

[79] IFC 1506:149, collected by James Delaney from John Naughton, Aughmagree, Kilteevan, Co. Roscommon, Feb. 1958.

[80] IFC 1550:70.

[81] IFC 1550:68-9, collected by James Delaney from Mary Anne Hanley, Derraghmylan, Rooskey, Co. Roscommon, 1958.

[82] Christiansen, 'The Dead and the Living', 38.

[83] IFC 1639:166, collected by James Delaney from John Ledwidth, America, Moor, Co. Roscommon, Oct. 1962.

[84] IFC 1550:168, collected by James Delaney from Patrick Mac Donnell, Caltra, Co. Roscommon, 1958.

[85] IFC 1575:502-4, collected by James Delaney from Kieran Mac Manus, Nure, Co. Roscommon, Feb. 1962.

[86] Ibid., 502.

[87] G. Ó Crualaoich, 'The Production and Consumption of Sacred Substances in Irish Funerary Tradition', 47.

[88]   IFC 1507:430, collected by James Delaney from James Grady, Rinnagan, St. John's, Co. Roscommon, Nov. 1958.

[89]   IFC 1781:72, collected by James Delaney from James Maxwell, Woodbrook House, Cootehall, Co. Roscommon, 1970.

[90]   IFC 1639:163, collected by James Delaney from John Ledwidth, America, Moor, Co. Roscommon, Oct. 1962.

[91]   IFC 1487:409, collected by James Delaney from Eugene Clarke and James Nolan, Ohill, Killoe, Co. Longford, Dec. 1957.

[92]   IFC 1676:36, collected by James Delaney from John Purcell, Money, Kilcormac, Co. Offaly, 1963.

[93]   IFC 1640:306, collected by James Delaney from William Talbot, ,Kilcormac, Co. Offaly, Nov.1963.

[94]   Cáit Ní Bhrádaigh, 'Folklore from Co. Longford', Béaloideas 6 (1936), 257-69; 261.

[95]   IFC 1550:238, collected by James Delaney from Ellen Hogan, Four Roads, Co. Roscommon, Sept. 1960.

[96]   Ó Crualaoich, 'The Production and Consumption of Sacred Substances in Irish Funerary Tradition', 46-7.

[97]   IFC 1736:28, collected by James Delaney from Patrick Doolin, Annagh, Ballykieran, Co. Westmeath, Autumn 1966.

[98]   IFC 195:113, collected by Pádraig Ó Ceannaigh from Eoghan Ó Nualláin, Urlár, Co. Maigh Eo, 1936.

[99]   IFC 1575:58-9, collected by James Delaney from Patrick Stephens, Ballyduff, Co. Galway, August 1960.

[100] IFC 1550:31, collected by James Delaney from John Flanagan, Mount Talbot, Co. Roscommon, June 1959.

[101] IFC 1506:538, collected by James Delaney from Mrs. Kate Ward, Corra More, Athleague, Co. Roscommon, 1958.

[102] IFC 1551:388, collected by James Delaney from John Gately (Senior), Coolegarry, Castletown, Co. Roscommon, Feb. 1960.

[103] IFC 1507:429, collected by James Delaney from James Grady, St. John's, Co. Roscommon, Nov. 1958.

[104] Isaac Weld, Statistical Survey of the County of Roscommon, Dublin 1832, 511.

[105] IFC 1536:161-3, collected by James Delaney from John Naughton, Aughmagree, Kilteevan, Co. Roscommon,1959.

[106] IFC 1575:507, collected by James Delaney from Kieran Mc Manus, Nure, Co. Roscommon, Feb.1962.

[107] IFC 1507:171-2, collected by James Delaney from Patrick Mc Govern, Swanlinbar, Co. Cavan, 1958.

[108] F. Coyne, 'Knockcroghery Clay Pipes', Roscommon Historical and Archaeological Society Journal I (1986), 45-46.

[109] IFC 1506:224-5, collected by James Delaney from John Stroker, Kilteevan Co. Roscommon, Spring 1958.

[110] IFC 1526:156-7, collected by James Delaney from Charles Furey, Mountplunket, Co. Roscommon, Feb. 1960.

[111] IFC 1506:224, James Delaney.

[112] IFC 1550:181, collected by James Delaney from Martin Nolan, Lissavruggy, Ballygar, Co Galway, 1958.

113 IFC 1506:539, collected by James Delaney from Mrs. Kate Ward, Corra More, Athleague, Co. Roscommon, 1959.

114 IFC 1550: 238, collected by James Delaney from Ellen Hogan, Four Roads, Co. Roscommon, Sept. 1959.

115 IFC 1575:450, collected by James Delaney from James Flynn, Clonown, Co. Roscommon, Jan. 1962.

116 IFC 1677:368, collected by James Delaney from Thomas Horan, Ballyduff, Co. Offaly, May 1963.

117 IFC 1487:408, collected by James Delaney from Eugene Clarke and James Nolan, Ohill, Co. Longford, Dec. 1957.

118 Ó Crualaoich, 'The Production and Consumption of Sacred Substances in Irish Funerary Tradition', 46.

119 Van Gennep, *The Rites of Passage*, 29.

120 IFC 1506:251, collected by James Delaney from Joseph Hanley, Clooneigh, Fourmile House, Co. Roscommon, March 1958.

121 IFC 1677:368, collected by James Delaney from Thomas Horan, Ballyduff, Co. Offaly, 1963.

122 IFC 1781:244, footnote added by James Delaney, Folklore Collector.

123 IFC 1550:31-34, collected by James Delaney from John Flanagan, Mount Talbot, Co. Roscommon, June 1958.

124 IFC 1487:90-1, collected by James Delaney from Mary Anne Hanley, Derraghmylan, Rooskey, Co. Roscommon, Nov. 1957.

125 IFC 1640:187, collected by James Delaney from Thomas Lucas, Clonfert, Co. Galway, May 1963.

126 IFC 1550: 176, collected by James Delaney from Patrick Mac Donnell, Caltra, Co. Roscommon, 1958.

127 IFC 1526:156, collected by James Delaney from Charles Furey, Mountplunket, Co. Roscommon, Feb. 1959.

128 IFC 1507:170, recorded by James Delaney from Patrick Mc Govern, Swanlinbar, Co. Cavan, 1958.

129 IFC 1575:508-9, collected by James Delaney from Kieran Mc Manus, Nure, Co. Roscommon, March 1962.

130 IFC 1506:538-9, collected by James Delaney from Mrs. Kate Ward, Corra More, Athleague, Co. Roscommon, 1958.

131 IFC 1575:444, recorded by James Delaney from James Flynn, Clonown, Co. Roscommon, Jan. 1962.

132 IFC 1551:158, recorded by James Delaney from James Nolan, Curraghcott, Tissrara, Co. Roscommon, Dec. 1959.

133 S Ó Súilleabháin, *Irish Wake Amusements*, 174. Morris, 'Irish Wake Games', 140.

134 IFC 1506:545, collected by James Delaney from Mrs. Kate Ward, Corra More, Athleague, Co. Roscommon, 1958.

135 W. G. Wood-Martin, *Traces of the Elder Faiths Of Ireland: A Folklore Sketch*, New York 1970, 314.

136 IFC 1506:145, collected by James Delaney from John Naughton, Aughmagree, Kilteevan, Co. Roscommon, Feb. 1958.

[137] S.J. Connolly, *Priests and People in Pre-Famine Ireland 1780-1845,* New York 1982, 152.

[138] Lady Wilde, *Ancient Cures, Charms and Usages of Ireland,* London 1890, 135.

[139] Morris, 'Irish Wake Games', 130-7.

[140] W. Carlton, 'Larry M'Farland's Wake', in *Traits and Stories of the Irish Peasantry,* New York 1979, 157-216; 201-2.

[141] IFC 1550:182-3, collected by James Delaney from Martin Nolan, Liosavruggy, Ballygar, Co. Galway, 1958.

[142] IFC 1839:125-6, James Delaney, 1973.

[143] IFC 1526:236, collected by James Delaney from Michael Gilligan, Cornageer, Cam, Co. Roscommon, March 1959.

[144] IFC 1550:190, collected by James Delaney from Martin Nolan, Lissavruggy, Ballygar, Co. Galway, 1959

[145] IFC 1550: 163-4, collected by James Delaney from Patrick Mac Donnell, Caltra, Co. Roscommon, 1959.

[146] Morris, 'Irish Wake Games', 129.

[147] IFC 1457:48, collected by James Delaney from Patrick Reilly, Enaghan, Granard, Co. Longford, 1956.

[148] IFC 1399:653, collected by James Delaney from Mrs. Margaret Rogers, Aughintemple, Co. Longford, Aug. 1955.

[149] Note: for movements of these games see Irish Wake Amusements, 41-115.

[150] IFC 1506:229-235, collected by James Delaney from John Stroker, Kilteevan, Co. Roscommon, March 1958.

[151] IFC 1526:237-8, collected by James Delaney from Michael Gilligan, Cornageer, Cam, Co. Roscommon, March 1959.

[152] IFC 1507:70-1, collected by James Delaney from James Milton, Bohy, Gortlettera, Co. Leitrim, July 1958.

[153] Ó Súilleabháin, *Irish Wake Amusements,* 102-3.

[154] IFC 1550:162-5, collected by James Delaney from Patrick Mac Donnell, Caltra, Co. Roscommon, 1959.

[155] IFC 1506:147-8, collected by James Delaney from John Naughton, Aughmagree, Kilteevan, Co. Roscommon, Feb. 1958.

[156] IFC 1781:27, recorded by James Delaney from James Maxwell, Woodbrook House, Cootehall, Co. Roscommon, May 1970.

[157] IFC 552:338-341, collected by Bríd Ní Ghamhnáin at Ballindoon, Boyle, Co. Roscommon, 1938.

[158] IFC 1399:514-5, collected by James Delaney from Frank Mc Naboe, Rossduff, Co. Longford, July 1955.

[159] IFC 1573:27-8, collected by James Delaney from John Gately, Coolagarry, Castletown, Co. Roscommon, March 1960.

[160] IFC 1506:237, collected by James Delaney from John Stroker, Kilteevan, Co. Roscommon, Spring 1958.

[161] IFC 1575:555, recorded by James Delaney from Mrs. Theresa Feeney, Tully, Killeroran, Co. Galway, April 1962.

[162] IFC1506:541-3, collected by James Delaney from Mrs. Kate Ward, Corra More, Athleague, Co. Roscommon, 1958.

[163] Morris, 'Irish Wake Games', 130, 139.

[164] IFC 1676:36, collected by James Delaney from John Purcell, Money, Kilcormac, Co. Offaly, Sept. 1963.

[165] IFC 1506:542, collected by James Delaney from Mrs. Kate Ward, Corra More, Athleague, Co Roscommon, Spring 1958.

[166] IFC 1506:228-9, collected by James Delaney from John Stroker, Kilteevan, Co. Roscommon, March 1958.

[167] IFC 1783:82, recorded by Michael Murphy from Michael Laughlin, Cleen, Dromahair, Co. Leitrim, 1973.

[168] IFC 552:337, recorded by Bríd Ní Ghamhnáin at Ballindoon, Boyle, Co. Roscommon, 1938.

[169] IFC 1677:287-8, collected by James Delaney from Tom Daly, Ballyduff, Co. Offaly 1963.

[170] IFC 1574:528, James Delaney, 1961.

[171] IFC 1639:265, collected by James Delaney from John Kenny, Newtown, Kiltoom. Co. Roscommon, 1962.

[172] IFC 1574:545-6, collected by James Delaney from Thomas Kelly, Dundonnell, Taughmaconnell, Co, Roscommon, Aug. 1961.

[173] Morris, 'Irish Wake Games', 130.

[174] IFC 1457:63, collected by James Delaney from Patrick Reilly, Enaghan, Dromard, Co. Longford, Feb. 1956.

[175] IFC 1796:290, collected by James Delaney from William Egan, Clonfanlough, Co. Offaly, 1973.

[176] Connolly, *Priests and People in Pre-Famine Ireland*, 160.

[177] Ibid., 164.

[178] IFC 1834:209-10, recorded by James Delaney from John Kenny, Kiltoom, Co Roscommon, 1973.

[179] IFC 1506:238, collected by James Delaney from John Stroker, Kilteevan, Co. Roscommon, Spring 1958.

[180] IFC 1640:305, collected by James Delaney from William Talbot, Kilcormac, Co. Offaly, Nov. 1963.

[181] Morris, 'Irish Wake Games', 129.

[182] IFC 1550:32, collected by James Delaney from John Flanagan, Mount Talbot, Co. Roscommon, June 1959.

[183] IFC 1677:120, collected by James Delaney from William Talbot, Kilcormac, Co. Offaly, 1963.

[184] IFC 1834:229, James Delaney, Kiltoom, Co. Roscommon, June 1974.

[185] Ariès, *The Hour of our Death*, 571.

Chapter Three

Burial

What funerals are really about is a common human dignity,
a worthwhile celebration of humanness, the statement of a
person's value and worth, an existential landmark locating
the dead in space and time and dividing the living from the
dead.[1]

In Ireland, traditionally burial took place on the third
day, following the wake of two nights' duration. Burial
took place in the late afternoon or evening; most folklore
accounts refer to it being about 3 or 4 o'clock. The period
between death and burial was a transitional one, marked
by rituals at various key points: in coffining of the body,
removing it from the house, the journey to the graveyard
and the actual burial. In traditional belief it was
important to adhere to particular customs during this
transitional period. As van Gennep writes:

Danger lies in transitional states, simply because transition
is neither one state nor the next, it is undefinable. The
person who must pass from one to another is himself in
danger and emanates danger to others. The danger is
controlled by ritual which precisely separates him from his
old status, segregates him for a time and then publicly
declares his entry to his new status.[2]

Rites of separation are in evidence in the different
procedures followed out to ensure that the deceased was
not hindered in his or her passage from this world to the
next. This chapter discusses some of the main rituals
recorded in folklore accounts for the midlands relating
to mass in the house, coffining the corpse, removal from
the house, bier/bearers, the route to the graveyard, the
grave and associated customs.

Mass and Funeral Offerings

Mass was said in the corpse house until the 1920s, in the
midlands, according to the folklore material
investigated. When it became obligatory to bring the
corpse to the chapel the night before burial, the practice

of having Mass in the house of the deceased was discontinued.

> The morning of the funeral, the priest of the parish used to come to say Mass in the house. The floor might not be swept, the fox herra would still be there after the game the night before, and an odd man half boozed. So the priest condemned the saying of Mass in the house and said it wasn't respectful. So for the last forty years Mass for the dead person is no longer said in the house but in the chapel.[3]

Most of the older narrators remembered the priest reading Mass in the kitchen on the day of the funeral. When John Gately's father died, there was Mass in his home at Castletown, south Roscommon, for him. 'They used to have Mass in the corp' house about forty or fifty years ago, but Mass is said in the Chapel now. The Mass was said in the kitchen of the corp' house, on the morning of the day of burial'.[4] According to Michael Gilligan of Cam, County Roscommon, before the priest said Mass:

> He would first ask if any young women had been at the wake the previous night, i.e. young women other than close relatives of the deceased. If he heard that any young women attended, who were not relatives, he would refuse to say Mass.[5]

Mass in the corpse house was not a universal practice however. In the village of Kilclough, northeast Galway: 'There never was the custom in this area of saying mass in the corpse house on the morning of the day of burial'. John Noone, the narrator, said he never even heard of it.[6] A custom recorded in the Parish of Moate, Westmeath, which was not mentioned in other folklore accounts investigated, concerned Mass on the morning of the day of burial: 'The water that the priest washed his hands in, at the Lavabo of the Mass, was handed around among the people to drink, when Mass was over. Any of the water that was left after this, was thrown on the fire'.[7]

Offerings (i.e. money donated voluntarily) were taken up by the priest after the mass or else he returned before the funeral left for the graveyard to collect the offerings. Most narrators in Roscommon do not remember offerings being collected in the Diocese of Elphin, but offerings were collected in the other dioceses in the midlands. An explanation for these 'offerings' was given by an informant in north Offaly:

> The offerin's were always taken up outside the door, in aul' times. That was the time before they started to bring the corpse to the chapel. They say it was the time of the Persecutions that the offerin's started. The only time they'd see a priest would be at a funeral. So when they'd see the priest at the funeral, they'd make a collection for him.[8]

In the parish of Gortlettera, County Leitrim it was recorded: 'It's only on account of the people that's livin' that offerings is paid. You pay offerings to show respect to them that the corpse belongs to and to show that you think well of them'.[9] An explanation for the collection of offerings found in other areas investigated was to help defray the funeral costs for families who were poor. Later, as people's circumstances changed, the money was given to the priest. Offerings were taken up at the church when the custom of bringing the deceased to the church overnight was introduced. In south Roscommon it was recorded that 'there are offerings still here in Clonown. Half a crown is what they pay. Me mother died in '58; she lived to be ninety eight, if you saw the table of offerings was at her funeral'.[10] In Longford:

> A table used to be brought out on the street outside the house and the offerin's would be lifted there, before the corpse would be brought out. The priest wouldn't go to the churchyard, but he'd bless the clay and then go home. The clay would be put in the coffin, after the priest blessin' it.[11]

If the priest did not attend the burial it was customary for him to bless clay which would be placed in the coffin or brought to the grave. In north Roscommon, the priest always went to the cemetery:

> In this Diocese of Elphin, he always went (i.e. to the graveyard). But in the Diocese of Ardagh and Clonmacnoise, in olden days, he blessed the clay an' he sent it with someone to the grave. He never went.[12]

In north Offaly, the narrator remembered going to the priest several times to get clay blessed.

The priest never went to the cemetery in aul' times, but when they started bringin' the corpse to the chapel, the priest began to go to the cemetery. What they used to do in aul' times someone would bring a pound paper bag with a handful of clay into the priest, before the body was coffined. The priest would bless the clay and that clay was put in the coffin.[13]

In later accounts from the Diocese of Ardagh and Clonmacnoise, the priest did attend the burial e.g. it was recorded in the Parish of Moate: 'As a rule the priest went to the churchyard to read the prayers over the grave. If he didn't go he'd bless clay and they'd put it in the coffin'.[14] In east Galway the custom was different, the clay was brought from the grave but it was not put in the coffin.

I heard me grandmother say that in olden days, the priest used not go to the graveyard for the funeral. Someone would go to the grave and get a handful or two of clay and bring it to the priest, and he would bless it. Then on the day of the funeral someone brought this clay to the graveside and threw it in to the grave on top of the coffin; three pieces of clay were thrown in, in the name of the Father, and of the Son and of the Holy Ghost.[15]

Coffining the Corpse
The coffin was left outside the front door of the house on its end until shortly before coffining took place, when it was brought head first into the house. Particular rituals were observed when the corpse was being placed in the coffin and these were similar in all the counties investigated. In south Roscommon, 'the people that leave out the corpse for the wake have to be there for the coffinin', as well. The people of the house, where the dead person is waked, would think it unlucky for you not to be there for the coffinin'.[16] It was customary to say the Rosary before the corpse was placed in the coffin:

All those present in the house kneel and say the Rosary. Then the coffining of the remains takes place. The same three women, who did the leaving out, also had to be present at the coffining. A man assisted at the coffining, as the women would not be able to do it on their own.[17]

In most of the accounts studied the three who laid out the corpse had to be present, although this practice is not stressed in all the folklore accounts. 'A couple of women usually coffined the corpse and they'd have a man helping them. Some young man would lift the corpse into the coffin for the women and then they'd do the rest'.[18] It was very important to remove any pins or bindings used for dressing the corpse before it was placed in the coffin.

> Bhíodh na seandaoine an-chúramach i dtaobh ghléasadh an choirp nuair a bhítí á chur sa chónra. Ní fhágaidís aon snaidhm ná aon cheangal ar an aibíd a bhainfeadh ó lúth ná ó choisíocht an duine mhairbh sa saol eile.

> [Old people used to be very careful concerning the dressing of the body when they were putting it in the coffin. They wouldn't leave any knot or tying on the habit that would interfere with the movement or walking pace of the dead person in the next life].[19]

In south Roscommon it was customary that the person who had prepared the corpse should be present to cut the cords placed on the hands and feet.[20] The same custom was practised in north Offaly: 'Before putting him in the coffin, I'd take out a knife and cut the string tying the toes together'.[21] In north Galway:

> a sod of turf would be broken and bits of it put into the coffin along with the corpse. All the safety pins and needles that would be pinned to the sheets when a person was laid out would also be put in the coffin.[22]

Various measures were taken to ensure that the corpse rested peacefully, as restless spirits returned to haunt the living. A tradition recorded in northwest Roscommon was that:

> The people who place the body in the coffin, always try to arrange it in such a manner that it will rest comfortably, as it is believed that a body that is not placed correctly in the coffin will not rest in peace.[23]

In east Galway:

> In the old days a little bundle of hay was put in the coffin under the head and feet of the corpse, to keep it from moving about in the coffin. The rosary beads belonging to the dead person and sometimes a prayer book were also put in the coffin.[24]

In Longford, 'shavin's from the wood were always put into the coffin where the head and shoulders of the corpse would lie'.[25] A similar practice was observed in

Transylvania, pointing to a more widely spread European practice:

> When the coffin arrives it is readied. The mattress and pillow consist of shavings from the wood used to make the coffin. (People are cautioned not to use feathers, which are the normal stuffing for pillows; it is thought that in the next world the dead would have to chase after the feathers and could not rest).[26]

It has been widely attested that religious articles were placed with the corpse - Rosary beads, prayer books, medals, and scapulars, a practice that continues. The practice was not particular to Ireland, but was more universally observed, e.g. in parts of France:

> Familiar objects were commonly placed in the coffin with the body. With the advance of literacy missals became popular, and the rosaries and crucifixes held by the dead were also sealed in the coffin. Women would sometimes be buried with their jewels, men with a pipe or a bottle of wine and children with their toys.[27]

The practice of burying the dead with objects that they might find useful or pleasurable in the afterlife is an ancient one. Klesman suggests with reference to modern France:

> This custom does not necessarily imply a belief that the objects would actually be employed by the dead; their presence in the coffin and the grave can rather be seen in part as designed to present a final, comfortable impression to the living observers of the corpse.[28]

In the late nineteenth and early twentieth century, in rural Ireland, the grave goods were simple but nonetheless meaningful. In Sligo, 'about half a pint of whiskey and tobacco and his pipe and Rosary beads and scapulars' were put in the coffin with the deceased, and this custom was still observed in 1970.[29] An older custom observed in Sligo, which was not mentioned in material investigated in the other counties studied, was to scatter cut tobacco in the coffin. The narrator believed it was an old pisreóg 'to save them from swelling or something like that'.[30]

In Ballymoe, in 1938, it was recorded that a herdsman expressed a wish 'that his sheep crook be placed beside him in the coffin. It is his belief that the soul of the Herdsman goes straight to Heaven'.[31] Most of the objects placed in the coffin in the early twentieth century had a religious significance and it is still customary, among Catholics, to have Rosary beads buried with the deceased. Flowers were sometimes used when the deceased was young and some of the flowers were put into the coffin.[32] Stockings and a hood/cap for the head were usually placed on the corpse immediately before coffining.

Traditionally coffining was one of the key times when lamentation over the corpse took place. 'It was vital according to folk belief that no tears fell on the corpse during lamenting, especially when the body was in the coffin'.[33] In the folklore material examined for the midlands the older narrators remembered keening at wakes and funerals when they were young. In Kilteevan, east Roscommon, the narrator remembered one particular occasion at a funeral:

> It was before the time they started bringin' the corpse to the chapel. I went in on the street and they brought out two chairs and then brought out the coffin and put it on the two chairs. There was two women standin' near the coffin and suddenly without any warnin' the two of them let out the damnedest cries out of them, ever you heard and frightened the heart out of me.[34]

On the Roscommon/Sligo border it was recorded in 1938: 'Lamenting for the dead is not carried out nowadays as it was long ago, in fact people do not try to show any more sign of grief than would be natural for them, either at a wake or a funeral'.[35]

The family and close relatives were usually left on their own with the deceased before the lid was placed on the coffin. The carpenter or handyman, who made the coffin, would have already placed nails in the lid so it was not necessary for him to be present. Placing and securing the lid on the coffin marked the physical separation of the deceased from the living. 'The nailing-down process represents the rather violent transformation of an important threshold into a permanent boundary'.[36] In later years screws were used in place of nails and the undertaker closed the coffin when the family had left the room. Richardson points out that:

Until this moment most of the customs associated with the body were home based and largely female in character. Washing and laying out were traditionally done by women, as were the dressing and binding. The nailing down of the coffin lid was done by the coffin-maker or undertaker, and presaged the onset of the public and more male-dominated part of the proceeding: the funeral itself.[37]

Removal from the House

Rites of separation which van Gennep called 'preliminal rites' were enacted as the corpse was carried across the threshold. These were conducted in a ritual manner as this period was seen as a time of danger for the living and the dead.

> The door is the boundary between the foreign and domestic worlds in the case of an ordinary dwelling, between the profane and sacred worlds in the case of a temple. Therefore to cross the threshold is to unite oneself with a new world.[38]

In Transylvania to prevent the return of the "living dead" (who are unnatural) 'as soon as the casket is beyond the threshold, the door is shut three times for good measure'.[39] In Denmark, as the corpse was being carried out:

> the bearers, just within the threshold of the door, raised and lowered it three times in different directions to form a cross. When the coffin had left the house, all chairs or stools on which it had rested were upset, all jars and saucepans turned upside down.[40]

As Fielberg points out:

> The cross formed by raising and lowering the coffin within the threshold, closes the doorway. Chairs and stools are upset so that he may find nothing to sit upon. For fear that the soul should remain behind, and hide in an empty jar, the vessels are all turned upside down.[41]

In the folklore material studied in the midlands the same mix of Christianity and superstition can be discerned. The Rosary was always said before the deceased was removed from the house and holy water was sprinkled as a safeguard against evil spirits. Some of the folklore accounts described chairs and sometimes tables being overturned and ascribed the same reason as is found internationally. In east Galway: 'Before the people left the house all the chairs were turned over, with their seats facing the floor. The belief was that the spirit of the dead person will walk round the place before the corpse is taken away'. This custom was still practised in the Menlough area, in the 1960s.[42] In Nure, south Roscommon: 'In former times when the corpse was laid out on a table in the kitchen, the table was turned upside down, as soon as the corpse was coffined'.[43] Often the narrators did not know why these customs were observed, it was sufficient to know that they were a tradition and as such had meaning and must be upheld.

Feilberg referred to the custom in Denmark of having a 'corpse door' in the old traditional houses which were built of bricks. 'In olden days it had been the custom that the coffin, which was always placed in the upper room, was carried out through this opening, which was bricked up again as soon as the procession had started for the church'.[44] In the folklore accounts studied, the houses were usually two or three roomed single storey traditional houses, and the coffin was carried out through the front doorway. In the case of two storey houses sometimes the procedure was different:

> Sometimes they have to take a coffin out through the top bedroom window. Usually when a corpse is waked upstairs or in the room (off the kitchen) it is awkward to bring a coffin to either room, so they bring the corpse in a sheet to the kitchen and coffin it there.[45]

Whiskey was given to those who coffined the corpse and usually porter was offered to the men who attended the house for the burial. 'There used to be porter at all the funerals and is yet. It is handed out at the room window. Four or five fellows would be watchin' the people arrive from every direction for to bring them up to get the porter'.[46] Clay pipes were left outside so that people could help themselves: 'The skibs would be left out on the wall, full of pipes, filled with tobacco, for everyone that came to the funeral'.[47] The removal did not take place until late afternoon; it was usually three or four o'clock when the deceased left the house for the graveyard.

The corpse was carried feet first from the house and this remained the position on the way to the cemetery. This practice has been widely attested in Irish folklore and in the tradition of other countries. 'The intention appears to have been to reinforce the funeral as a one way journey to disposal, deliberately designed to remain unidirectional'.[48] In folklore tradition in the midlands, four of the same name carried the coffin from the house; and this custom continued in some areas until the 1960s at least:

> Four people-men-of the same surname as the dead person, were sought to take out the remains from the house. It could be four cousins, or four sons or four nephews, the name was more important than the relationship. This custom is still held to strictly.[49]

In Athleague in 1958, it was recorded:

> At one time four men of the same name as the dead person had to carry out the coffin from the house to the street outside. The men had to be of the same surname. If possible the rule is still kept to the present day, though it is not so easy nowadays, with such a scattering on the people, to get four of the same name.[50]

It was customary according to all the folklore studied to rest the coffin on chairs outside the door, for a short period of time, before leaving for the graveyard. In northwest Roscommon it was recorded that 'four chairs are placed outside the door and the coffin is left resting on them for a few minutes'.[51] The latter is the only reference to four chairs being used. According to James Flynn of Clonown, in south Roscommon, 'the aul' chairs that they had long ago were big and strong and you'd only want two of them'.[52] In most accounts two chairs were used:

> It was the custom to place the coffin on two chairs, one end of the coffin on the seat of each chair. The coffin was allowed to rest on the chairs for just a few seconds and then taken up again. As soon as the coffin was taken up the chairs were knocked down, kicked over, so that the back of the chair fell forward on the ground.[53]

In folklore accounts recorded in the midlands, in all the dioceses except Elphin, the offerings were taken up by the priest at this point and this sometimes determined the length of time that the coffin remained on the chairs. The custom of leaving the coffin on chairs outside the house has been widely attested, and they were always knocked over once the coffin was raised from them. If this were not done there might be another death in the family. Similar rituals were practised on the Islands in Lough Ree, some of which were populated until the middle of the twentieth century: 'The chairs are placed facing each other and the coffin is placed on the seats of the chairs, the head on one seat and the feet on another'.[54] In Nure, south Roscommon, a different practice was observed: 'The chairs were first put face downwards and the coffin was placed on the back legs and someone stood near to see that the chairs did not over balance'.[55]

Rice, a local author, refers to the old belief that a corpse left on a flagstone beside Portlick on the Longford shore of Lough Ree, would float out for burial by the monks on the islands. 'The stone would move and float out across the waters to Inis Cleraun or Inis Ainghin, and there the monks would take him and give him Christian burial'.[56] In folklore James Delaney collected in Longford, in the late 1950s, there are references to particular flagstones which had been used in association with burial at early Christian sites on islands. However the flagstones only survive in folk memory because someone usually interfered with them or desecrated them in some way which caused them to disappear. James Farrell, who was reared on Inchcleraun, had heard about the flagstone from his grandfather:

> It was on the shore on Saints' Island, and when a corpse would come to the mainland shore the flag would move out in the lake and over to the mainland and they'd put the corpse on the flag and the flag would move back to the Saints' Island, where there was a cemetery. A woman washed clothes on the flag and didn't the flag move out into the Lake and disappeared.[57]

Teampall na Marbh, Saints' Island, Lough Ree

Saints' Island

He was also told by his grandfather that it was usual at one time to put the coffined corpses of people about to be buried in the ruins of one of the church buildings on Inchcleraun, called the house of the dead. He was not sure if they were left overnight or not, but before burial they were placed in the church ruins.[58]

Teampall na Marbh/Church of the Dead, Inchcleraun

Inchcleraun

According to Kate Flood of Columcille parish, Longford, people 'used to come far and near to bury their dead in Inch Island' (Inchmore, Lough Gowna).[59] An account concerning a flagstone on Inchmore and burial is very similar to the previous account about Saints' Island.

> There used to be a big green flagstone on the island and when people from the mainland would be bringin' in a corpse to be buried, this flagstone used to move out from the island to the mainland. They would put the coffin on the stone and it would bring the coffin over to the island and the stone would stop there, on the shore, for the next burial.[60]

When boats were used to take people from the islands on Lough Ree for burial on the mainland the following was the procedure, according to James Farrell:

> The coffin is carried down to the boat, feet foremost, and the boat is already placed at the pier, with its bow facing the mainland, and the coffin is placed in the boat, usually on two chairs, still feet foremost, that is with the feet facing the bow or the stem of the boat and the head pointing in the direction from which the funeral has come.[61]

Those who lived beside the Shannon, in south Roscommon, liked to be buried in Clonmacnoise because it was believed that 'anyone who is buried in the Seven Churches will go to Heaven'. A special boat or 'cot' was used in this area of the Shannon. 'The coffin would be put feet first into the cot and all the funeral would be brought over in cots then, and they'd l'ave the coffin on the bank and go over for the rest of the funeral, until they were all brought over'.[62] It was more convenient for people to use boats if the burial grounds were close to the banks of the Shannon, as many families who lived close to the river owned boats. John Connaughton remembered his grandfather's funeral being taken over to Woodbank Callas:

They took up the Shannon to Shannonbridge. Funerals used often to cross the Shannon like that. The coffin would be put in a boat, with two men rowin'. The feet of the coffin would face the bow of the boat.[63]

Joseph Hanley's description of a funeral he attended from Inch Éanach is similar:

I went to a funeral in Inch Éanach one time and they say that never a funeral left there but the wind rose. And we went into a pub on the Longford side; it was Farrells and we could only take a standin' dram in it. Everyone could only take one drink in it and then go. The funeral went to the Parish of Cashel. It was a very big funeral. Every boat from around the shore was in it. There was one boat for the coffin, with a couple of men to row it. The coffin is always placed with the feet facin' the stem, and it is rowed out feet first, all the time.[64]

When boats were used for transport the remains were accompanied by next of kin. Four of the same name, who need not necessarily be relatives, carried the coffin to the boat and again from it when they reached their destination.

Bier/Bearers

A beir or bearer was used to carry the coffin before the introduction of horses and carts. The bearer used to transport the coffin according to the folklore accounts was a simple stretcher made of timber. 'The bearers were two long poles about nine or ten feet long, with laths nailed across them, and they used to tie the coffin on to the bearer'.[65] Sometimes the carpenter made the bearer when he was making the coffin. In north Offaly he charged nothing for making it but the timber 'would cost that time anything between five an' seven bob'.[66] Most accounts describe the coffin being borne on a bearer but Michael Gilligan, of Curraghboy, south Roscommon, who was aged 92 years, in 1959, saw sheets being used:

They used to put sheets in under the handles of the coffin and carry them that way. They carried an aul' woman that died here, from here to Rahara that way. I was there myself and helped to carry. Then they used to have bearers – two sticks – and they'd carry the coffin on the sticks on their shoulders. It was a kind of honour for the dead to carry them.[67]

Another older narrator also saw sheets being used to carry the coffin:

> Two sheets were twisted and put through the handles of the coffin, and underneath the coffin. The ends of the sheets were knotted and the men carrying the coffin, carried it by the aid of the sheets. The coffin was carried about knee high.[68]

In the late 1950s it was recorded in east Galway that 'the oldest method of attending a funeral was by walking after it, with men carrying the coffin on their shoulders or with the aid of sheets'.[69]

The bearers were changed according to a set ritual and this was widely attested in all the folklore material investigated for the midland counties. Kieran Mc Manus of Nure, south Roscommon, described it thus:

> They'd take turns to carry the coffin, when two new men would be takin' their turn, they'd go to the front (under the foot of the coffin) and the two men in front would fall behind and take the place of the men at the back, and them two back men would fall out and join the funeral.[70]

John Devery aged 87 years, of Lecarrow, County Offaly, described a similar exchange of places among men carrying the coffin on bearers to Clonmacnoise for burial.

> Four men would get in under the bearer, two in front and two behind and lift it on their shoulders. And when they'd be changin', two new men would go in, in front and the two front men would go behind, and the two behind would drop out and join the funeral. And they'd be sure to match companions, so that every pair would be the same height.[71]

The coffin often had to be carried for a lengthy period of time as the graveyard might have been at a distance or a family might have had a tradition of burial in some particular place.

> Often your shoulders would be cut from carryin' the coffin on the bearers, when there wouldn't be many at the funeral. We often brought a coffin from here (i.e. Lecarrow) to Kilbegley, in the Parish of Moor, below in Roscommon [c. 6 miles if they crossed the Shannon].[72]

When Isaac Weld visited Rindoon to prepare his Statistical Survey of County Roscommon for the Royal Dublin Society in 1832, he commented on the practice of leaving biers on the graves as well as leaving bodies imperfectly interred:

> A custom also obtains, of which I do not recollect to have seen traces in any other place, of leaving on the graves rude biers, usually formed of saplings or green boughs, on which the bodies have been borne.[73]

It was customary according to the folklore investigated to break the bearer against a tombstone after the burial. 'The bearer was always broken against a headstone (in the graveyard) when they'd have the corpse brought to the churchyard'.[74] In most of the accounts it was left there because people were superstitious about bringing anything back from a graveyard. 'When they'd have the corpse buried, they'd get big stones and they'd break those bearers into small pieces within in the graveyard, so that nobody 'id turn them to any use. That was the custom'.[75]

There are a few references to people reusing bearers although generally it was not the rule. 'When they'd get to the graveyard they'd break the bearer again a headstone and l'ave it there. Some fellows would bring them and make a nice little ladder of them'.[76] In east Galway, the bearer was always broken because people were afraid another death might follow if it was not. Later 'they just broke off the lists or cross pieces, off the bearer, and someone used to come and make use of the wood to make a turf barrow or a gate'.[77]

In Kilcormac, County Offaly, the narrator refers to the bearer being reused for another funeral:

> The bearers were left in the cemetery in some sheltered place. Then the next funeral that come, a couple had to go to the cemetery and collect the bearer and bring it in. But the same bearer would last for years. All the poor of the town were carried on bearers and so were the gentry. It was supposed to be an honour for the gentry to be carried on bearers.[78]

There was a special custom recorded in 1938, in northwest Roscommon, for the funeral of a young unmarried boy or girl which involved their friends buying white calico, for use as scarves. 'They wear those scarves which are usually about six inches wide across the right shoulder when walking in the funeral procession'.[79] The same custom was observed in the late 1950s in southwest Roscommon:

> About twenty four or thirty young men would attend the funeral in a special manner. They would all wear big white scarves. These scarves, or sashes, were worn over the right shoulder and under the left arm and were tied at the hip with a big black bow. These young people would have charge of the funeral from the time that they put on the sashes. Four of them would carry the coffin, relieving one another two by two. One of them went out in front of the coffin, carrying a wreath. All the others carried sally rods, peeled, in their hands. The top of the rod was split and into this split was put a small piece of white paper, done in such a way that it had the appearance of a white rose.[80]

The same custom was recorded in Galway which involved twenty four young men forming a guard of honour.

> They march two and two, beside the coffin (or the hearse). They used to wear white sashes, but they wear white armlets now, and they each carry a white rod (a peeled sally rod) about two feet long. This happens in the case of a young boy or girl between sixteen and thirty years of age.[81]

A custom called "shifting the coffin" pertained in parts of the north of Ireland in the nineteenth century, which involved young women carrying a coffin: 'There was at one time, some forty or fifty years ago, a rather romantic custom, that when a very young unmarried woman died her coffin should be carried by young girls only to the graveyard'.[82]

Other Modes of Transport
The tradition of carrying the coffin on bearers to the graveyard began to die out at the beginning of the twentieth century and carts were then used to transport the coffin to the graveyard. In the folklore material investigated when a horse and cart were used to carry the coffin, the horse had to be valued.

> The horse goin' under the cart that was to carry the corpse to the churchyard had to be valued before the funeral started out. The man that owned the mare (or horse) would ask some man that'd be there, what was she worth? He'd say whatever price he'd like, forty pound, or fifty or whatever he thought the mare was worth. If the mare was not valued they used to say it was unlucky. She might die.[83]

In Galway also it was recorded that 'twelve men had to have a say' before the mare was allowed carry the corpse:

> In those times, fifty years ago, the coffin was carried on a common cart, with the farmer's own animal under the cart. Well, if the farmer had a brood mare, the mare would not be allowed to bring the coffin to the graveyard, unless twelve men decided that she should.[84]

In Galway and Roscommon similar beliefs were recorded regarding the horse or mare. 'There's something about a brood mare', says Mrs Martin Nolan, 'and lots of people say, when the head of a house dies, that it's right to sell the brood mare'.[85] According to John Gately (Senior) of Curraghboy: 'It was the custom and some do it yet, to sell the horse, when the man of the house dies'.[86] Some people did not place much credence in these superstitions:

> They used to lament the horse was never any good after carrying a corpse, but I don't see what harm carryin' a corpse would do the horse. I carried many a one on th' aul' jinnet and he was never a bit the worst of it that I saw. When they'd be carrying the corpse on a cart, two women would be sittin' on the coffin.[87]

The tradition in some areas of the west of Ireland was for women, usually three, to sit on the coffin, when it was transported on a cart. The following was recorded by Ciarán Bairéad in the parish of Belclare, Galway:

> Formerly the coffin was taken for burial on a farm cart. Three women, two married and one single used to sit on the coffin, facing in different directions. The cart then moved forward for a small distance and halted. The horse was unyoked and turned completely round and then yoked again, two men supporting the shafts while this was being done. This was repeated three times, the horse being turned in a different direction each time, then the funeral finally moved off.[88]

The previous account would suggest that it was done to protect the deceased and avert evil on its final journey. In folklore recorded by James Delaney in the midlands, there are no references to women sitting on the coffin, in the folklore investigated, but people were aware that it was customary in Galway: 'In Galway some relative would have to sit on the coffin, as it was being brought for burial in a horse cart'.[89] The custom was observed by an Englishman at a funeral in Achill, northwest Mayo, in 1897:

> In the middle of the funeral train was one of the flat carts used in Connaught, with two short shafts for tilting purposes prominent behind, and on it the humble coffin of unplaned deal, with a sheet of paper – which may have borne the name and age of the deceased, with perhaps a prayer or two – tacked over the breast. The poorest Irish display an inordinate affection for their dead, and in Achill the nearest relatives testify their love and respect by sitting on the coffin during its progress to the graveyard.[90]

In most of the folklore accounts only one horse was involved when carts were used for transporting the deceased for burial, in rural areas. The circumstances of the deceased, and his or her family of course, often determined the type of transport used. There are descriptions of ornate horse drawn hearses when undertakers were employed.

> The farmers used to have a hearse, with four horses and the horses would have plumes out of them and the driver would have a caroline hat. Four horsemen, with caroline hats would escort the hearse. They'd ride at aitch corner of the hearse. The driver of the hearse would be in livery. He'd have a big blue topcoat and a caroline hat and a big white sash across his shoulder. The four horsemen beside the hearse also wore white sashes and caroline hats.[91]

Funeral of business man or strong farmer

In the midland counties hearses began to be used at the beginning of the twentieth century. Their use marked the end of the 'walking funerals' which had been a traditional feature of Irish funerary practice. In south Roscommon, Kieran Mc Manus remembered the last walking funeral at the turn of the century. 'Me father, Lord have mercy on him, was the last corpse to be carried to Drum from this village (i.e. Nure), sixty three years ago, last November. The hearses came after that'.[92] The following description was recorded of the first hearse used in Roscommon town: 'It was an awful black aul' thing, like a box on wheels and when the coffin would be put into it, you couldn't see it. They used put a white plume on it for a young unmarried person and a black plume for anyone else'.[93] When John Flanagan's mother died at Mount Talbot, in 1905, she had a hearse. 'It cost fifteen shillings to bring a hearse out from Roscommon to Mount Talbot'.[94] Hearses continued to be used throughout the twentieth century but the custom of four men carrying the coffin for a short distance remained. In Longford the following was recorded at a Traveller's funeral:

> Oney Power died in 1937 at Ballymahon and had an enormous funeral. Tinkers from all the surrounding counties attended. His relatives bought an expensive coffin, hired a hearse and carried the coffin behind an empty hearse almost two miles, to the lonely graveyard of Cloncallow on the banks of the Inny.[95]

Route to the Graveyard
The longest route was always taken to the graveyard and there were recognized stopping places along the way. This is widely attested in all the folklore investigated and it is recorded from other cultures also.

> The journey to the burial place was not always direct, and was occasionally punctuated by a series of stops – either by slowing down or pausing for a moment, or by stopping altogether for refreshment, prayers or singing. These stopping sites could be linear or associational.[96]

The custom of taking the longest route can be seen as an effort to placate the dead. Estyn Evans points out that:

The coffin was carried to the graveyard by the longest route, preferably a disused track, and the procession made a sunwise circle around some place or object, a cross, a church site, a lone thorn tree or a crossroads' with the object of deceiving the spirit of the dead.[97]

This idea is substantiated in folklore from the midlands: 'The funeral should take the longest way round to the churchyard. If that wasn't done they say the person would come back. Every funeral must take the longest route. This custom is still observed'.[98] The longer route was chosen too out of respect for the dead as people did not wish to give the impression that they were hurrying them to the grave. On the Roscommon/Galway border it was observed that: 'The coffin in the funeral procession is always taken by the old road – never taken by a shortcut or a new road to the graveyard'.[99] In Kiltoom, west of Athlone, the tradition of taking the old road continued until the 1960s, according to James Delaney: 'I was living in the district some ten years ago when the last burial took place to the old graveyard of Kiltoom inside Strevins's main entrance gate and it took the winding course of the old road, as was the custom'.[100]

In the material investigated the tradition of keening en route to the funeral continued into the twentieth century. Most of the older narrators described groups of women following the coffin, crying, on the way to the grave. As James Delaney pointed out the word keener was not used in the midlands, the usual word was 'crier'.

There used to be criers at funerals long ago. Women would cry after the corpse at the funeral from the house to the churchyard. These women wouldn't be relations of the dead person at all, but they'd be sent for by the relatives to come and cry at the funeral.[101]

Patrick Johnson

Patrick Johnson of Ballinlassie, County Westmeath, whose mother was a professional mourner, said they were sent for when someone died and she described the procedure to him. 'We'd all get four deep and we'd cry for about three hundred yards or four hundred yards from the house to the churchyard'.[102] John Lennon of Drum parish remembered keening en route to the graveyard. 'They used to come from Nure to be buried in Drum and they used to carry the coffin on their shoulders, and they'd be cryin'. The friends belongin' to the corpse would cry the corpse the whole way nearly'.[103] Patricia Lysaght points out that folklore accounts indicate 'that the lament was performed at locations *en route* where the funeral procession traditionally halted, or where the coffin was formerly placed while the bearers rested'.[104] In Roscommon there are two particular placenames which have traditionally been associated with keening. 'At Rathcroghan, outside Reilig na Rí enclosure there is a mound called 'Cnocán na gCorp' [Hill of the Bodies.] Local tradition says corpses were laid here to be keened over before burial'.[105] In south Roscommon, Ardkeenan has been associated with keening in folklore from early times:

In aulden times, when they'd be buryin' the O'Connor Kings in Clonmacnoise, they used to come down from the North through Drum, and when they'd come to the Hill of the Cry, they'd see Clonmacnoise for the first time and they'd raise the cry there. (Collectors note: The local name for this hill is Ardkeenan, but old people sometimes translate the Irish of Ardkeenan into the Hill of the Cry). Ardkeenan has given its name to the townland in which it is situated.[106]

Kieran Mc Manus

Kieran Mc Manus, whose family originally came from the north of Ireland, referred to a custom of funerals stopping overnight at a dead or wake house:

> They carried the coffin the whole way from the North. And if they weren't able to get over to Seven Churches before night, they'd stop here (in Nure) and wait for the next day, and they'd leave the corpse in the dead house above.[107]

This is the only reference in the folklore investigated to an actual wake house, but, according to tradition a cabin situated beside Mc Manus's house and the field where it stood were known as keening locations.[108] James Delaney pointed out that Mc Manus was the sole surname in Nure and the families were all related. 'All the Mc Manuses in Nure came from the North, and they settled in Nure and Ardnanure. They were put out of the North when they were fighting in the North hundreds of years ago'.[109] At the end of the eighteenth century, many Catholics were expelled from Ulster and they settled in Connaught. Many of them were weavers and linen workers and they brought their trades with them.[110] Tohall refers to a pre-arranged sectarian combat, 'The Diamond Fight' of 1795, which was made:

> the pretext for the violent expulsion of ten thousand Catholics, or more, the majority of whom sought refuge in Connaught. The numerous Mac Manus homes between Athlone and Ballinasloe claim Fermanagh origin of this period.[111]

This may explain the use of a designated wake house for funerals from Ulster in this area of south Roscommon in the nineteenth century.

The tradition of the funeral procession stopping at particular places en route to the graveyard was widely attested in the folklore material, especially on the 'Pilgrims' Road' to Clonmacnoise. This route is described by Peter Harbison, archaeologist, as 'prime among the shorter pilgrimage roads'.[112] According to tradition, the Pilgrims' Road was part of the road which went from Longford to Clonmacnoise. Thomas Daly, described the route to James Delaney: 'It comes through Clooneyderg, Ballyduff, Cloonasra; it crosses the present main road from Ballinahown to Seven Churches (i.e. Clonmacnoise). It goes through the Hanging Hills, through Buntulla and into Seven Churches'.[113] All those places named lie between Daly's house and Clonmacnoise. Funerals coming for burial from Longford, Westmeath and Offaly came by this route and the informants were familiar with the customary stops.

Thomas Daly's house, along the Pilgrims' Road

On the three roads leading to Clonmacnoise, the road from Shannonbridge, the road that goes by Tully Hill and the road that goes through Cloonasra, on all these roads there was a special place (and still is) where a pause was made by funerals. Tradition says that the boundaries of the ancient monastery came to those three points on the three roads, respectively and that the lay people had to leave the coffins there in ancient times. The monks took the coffins from these places and brought them and buried them themselves.[114]

An explanation which John Connaughton of Lisduff, County Offaly, gave for funerals stopping at Buntolla, was:

Others say that the custom came from the time that the cholera was ragin' all over the country and Clonmacnoise was the only place that was free of it. So to keep the cholera from Clonmacnoise no one was let into the city beyond Buntulla, and that's why the coffins were taken from the people.[115]

Michael Shanny of Moor, south Roscommon, knew of a bush on the road to Clonmacnoise, and in olden times, nuns from Clonmacnoise, used to come to that point to take charge of the corpse for burial:

·They'd stand there with the corpse and the nuns used to come up to take the corpse from there to Clonmacnoise. And they'd carry the corpse down to the burial ground and make the grave and cover the grave. And the r'ason for this was for fear any sinner would put foot in the sacred soil.[116]

An older narrator, John Devery, aged 87 years in 1963, of Lecarrow, County Offaly, remembered carrying corpses on bearers from Shannonbridge to Clonmacnoise.

There was a place below on the road to Clonmacnoise and there was a bush growin' there – a whitethorn. We'd l'ave the coffin down there, on the road, at that bush. And we'd turn the coffin around with the feet facin' the way we came. And all would take off their hats then and say a few prayers. Then we'd take up the coffin and on again for the graveyard and there was another place, below that, and there was a stone and there was like an image on it. And we'd do the very same thing in that place, opposite the stone.[117]

The tradition of funerals stopping at special places along the route was upheld for many years and hearses still stopped for a moment there in the late twentieth century. As has already been mentioned those who lived beside the Shannon in south Roscommon crossed by boat to Clonmacnoise to bury their dead. 'Drumlosh and Curraghnabull all goes to Seven Churches (i.e. Clonmacnoise) to be buried'.[118] When the funeral reached the monastery there was a particular route that was taken whether they came by boat or road:

We'd go around the big cross – the Cross of the Scriptures they call it – and we'd go into the big Church – it's the biggest of the ruins there in the Churchyard – and we'd go in the west door with the corpse, and we'd let down the coffin, with the feet facin' where the High Altar was, and then we'd say prayers there. We'd bring the coffin on again out the north door and go ahead to the graveyard.[119]

Relatives taking the remains of Mick Shine, Drumlosh, to Clonmacnoise in 1939. Kieran McNeill is poling the Cot.

North Door of Cathedral, Clonmacnoise

Temple Ciarán, Clonmacnoise

The custom of funerals stopping to say prayers at crossroads or death cairns on route to the graveyard was recorded throughout the midlands. As Máire Nic Néill points out that places where deaths occurred in the open were often marked by a heap of stones or twigs or grass to which each passer-by added.

> Halts at special places during funeral processions were once common in Ireland and still survive in some districts. At some of them the coffin was laid down on a stone-heap while prayers were recited, and in some places refreshments were provided. The passer-by added his stone to the resting-place heap just as to a death heap.[120]

In the material investigated the custom of building 'stone heaps' to commemorate the dead was a common practice in Galway and Mayo and they have also been recorded in Sligo and Leitrim. The following information was recorded, in reply to the 1938-39 Questionnaire from the Folklore Commission, on the death-cairn custom:

> There are a few Stone Heaps about Arigna and on the Sligo Leitrim and Roscommon borders near Lough Allen, but they only mark Famine Graves (1846-47), and there is no local tradition about them and no stone has been added to them in years.[121]

A schoolgirl from Aughrim, described a custom her father witnessed at a funeral in Cloonfad, south Roscommon:

> As the coffin went on, the funeral followed, and went to a burying ground in Kilbegley. Midway between Kilbegley and Cloonfad, the cortege came to a bend on the road. There was a stone cross, and a fairly sized heap of loose stones, that were thrown on the side of the road around the cross. When the hearse came to the cross, it turned around the road once and the people followed it. My father asked a man the cause of this. He told him that there was a priest buried where the cross was, and that was the cause of all the turns at the cross.[122]

In south Leitrim it was recorded that 'heaps' are placed where they are to mark a sudden death; they do not mark a burial place nor do they mark where coffins rested. 'Funeral halts usually took place at crossroads. The bearers usually placed the coffin on some stones, for it was regarded and still is regarded as very wrong and unlucky to leave a coffin with a corpse in it on the clay (ground).[123] In Galway it was also customary to stop at crossroads.

> Ó Bhéal Cláir soir agus i bhfad níos fuide soir ná Tuaim, is ag na cros-bhóthair a stadadh said. Bhaineadh said an capall ón gcairt agus shiúbhaladh fear agus capall thart ar chairt is cónra, trí uaire.

> [From Belclare west and further west than Tuam, it was at the crossroads they stopped. They used to take the horse from the cart and the man and the horse would walk three times round the cart and coffin].[124]

In Ballymoe there were traditions concerning hawthorn bushes and death. A hawthorn bush marked the place where a woman named Dolly died, and for several generations afterwards 'people as they walked past Dolly's bush, picked from the road a small stone and threw it at the roots of the old bush'. No prayer was ever offered for Dolly because it was felt that she might have been murdered. Another hawthorn bush known as the 'Pooka Bush', planted where a young man met his death, had the same tradition but a prayer was added for him:

> Man, woman and child when passing the bush, picked from off the road a small stone and threw it under the bush repeating whilst doing so, "May the Lord have mercy on

the dead" – thus in time, a heap was formed under the bush.[125]

Neither of these sites were funeral stops which is unusual as in other counties they would have been. The narrator is quite definite that in this area of Roscommon-Galway there were no stops made: 'In this district and in surrounding districts funeral processions never halt, nor are coffins rested on the way to the graveyard. There are no wooden crosses erected to mark where funeral processions ever halted'.[126] Later on, in the twentieth century, crosses of wood or stone were erected to commemorate people who died on roadways. Sometimes a cross was drawn on a wall or marked out in grass and currently flowers or wreaths often mark the place of an accident.

A custom observed in the nineteenth century funerary practice in France is interesting because a similar custom is referred to in Ireland in two particular areas.

> Small wooden crosses, distributed by the family to the mourners, were placed at crossroads, where the procession would stop for a rest and a prayer for the deceased – a practice derived from the belief that the souls of the dead were drawn to these central spots.[127]

Margaret Stokes, art historian, points out that a similar tradition was found in Wexford and in Cong, on the Mayo/Galway border. Both of these areas were associated with Saint Fursy who had travelled to Picardy in France. In Wexford pieces of wood left over from making the coffin were made into small crosses.

> They have pointed shafts; and one which is meant to be planted in the soil at the head of the grave, is laid on the coffin, while the others are carried by the chief mourners behind. At the cross-roads nearest to the cemetery there is always a hawthorn tree, at the foot of which the procession pauses, and the cross bearers lift the crosses to its branches, where they fix them and leave them.[128]

On a visit to Cong with the Royal Society of Antiquarians she (Stokes) noticed the same custom at Cong. 'The general procession going to the old Abbey of Cong pauses at the last crossroads to deposit their crosses, but here the tree is an ash, not a thorn'.[129] The hawthorn tree is regarded as sacred in folklore because of its association with the 'Crown of Thorns'. In folklore in Kerry people were aware of the connection of the whitethorn with the Passion of Christ: 'A whitethorn stick is very bad, it is said that an animal never should be struck with it because it was of that tree the Crown of Thorns was made'.[130] At another site near Cong, on the Clonbur road, there is still a tradition of placing little crosses at a stone monument which has a plaque commemorating John and Mary Joyce who were murdered at this spot, on 6 August 1712.[131]

Joyce Monument, outside Cong

Respect for the dead was evident in all of the customs enacted on the journey to the graveyard. It was also necessary for those meeting a funeral to acknowledge it, either by walking part way with it or stopping and blessing themselves:

> The custom is that when one meets a funeral one should walk back three steps with it, 'what is called in Irish, *trí céimeanna na trócaire* - or the three steps of mercy'. A man called Daly neglected to do this and it was given as a reason for his death.[132]

In folklore in Longford the same tradition was held: 'A person meeting a funeral should always turn back and walk at least three steps with the funeral'.[133] In south Roscommon when people either walking or driving in a horse and cart met a funeral the following custom was observed: 'The driver always dismounted and removed his hat and walked six to eight paces in the direction the funeral was going'. Edward Egan's father 'kept up this tradition all his lifetime'.[134] In towns when a funeral was passing it was customary to close the doors of the shops and pull down blinds on windows until it had passed by. 'In Roscommon town some of the shops had special shutters which they placed on the windows, up to the late 1960s'.[135]

Grave

There were very strict regulations relating to the grave; when it could be opened, the placement of the coffin and of other interred bones and the filling in of the clay. Different rituals and customs were involved and superstitions upheld because this was the final rite of separation.

> The grave itself is the corpse's final threshold. Among the images which adorned seventeenth and eighteenth century funerary invitations were the crossed spade and pick, which echoed the old custom of protecting the threshold by leaving implements crossed over the threshold until its use.[136]

Usually some member of the family pointed out the family plot to the gravediggers or some older person who was knowledgeable about the graveyard. 'The owner of the grave goes to the graveyard the morning of the funeral to point out the grave to the people who are going to dig it and he brings a bottle of whiskey with him'.[137] Usually three men were involved in digging the grave, normally neighbours and sometimes a relation of the deceased, but never a father or brother. 'Three men would be told to make the grave the mornin' of the funeral, and then they'd get a pint of whiskey. They wouldn't touch the whiskey until after they'd dig the first sod'.[138] There were superstitions in some areas about opening a grave on a Monday e.g. in County Mayo:

Má tá sé riachtanach duine a chur Dea Luain is ceart an
uaigh a fhoscailt lá eicínt roimh an Luan ná ar an laghadh
ceithre fóda a thiompadh san áit a bhfuil dúil aca an uaigh a
fhoscailt

[If it is necessary to bury a person on a Monday it is right to
open the grave some day before or at least to turn four sods
in the place where they wish to open the grave].[139]

The same belief was recorded in the Parish of
Ballynahowan in Offaly and in the Parish of Moor in
Roscommon:

There is no openin' a grave on a Monday in this district. If a
man dies of a Saturday, they go and take a few scraws off
the grave of a Sunday evenin', and then they can say that
the grave was opened on a Sunday. They dig the rest of the
grave on Monday, the day of the funeral.[140]

In both counties it was stressed that the custom was
observed in the case of the head of the household. 'You
never open a grave for the head of the house of a
Monday. You could open it of a Sunday and then finish
it on Monday, but you couldn't open it on the
Monday'.[141] In Moor they circumvented the superstition
also by removing a sod on Sunday and the mother was
also regarded as the head of the house. 'A grave should
never be opened on a Monday for the head of a house,
for either the father or the mother'.[142] In Cloonkeenkerrill
in east Galway, the custom of avoiding burial on
Mondays is still observed. According to traditional belief
there was a dispute between Saint Kerrill and Saint
Connell, and Connell cursed Cloonkeenkerrill and said
that a corpse would be brought there for burial every
Monday:

Kerrill overcame the curse saying that the corpse would be
that of a starling, leading to the popular belief that a dead
starling can be found at Cloonkeenkerrill every Monday.
The practice of avoiding burials on Mondays is rigidly
observed in case Saint Connell's curse might be re-
established.[143]

In other areas investigated this custom did not apply,
you could open a grave any day. In Kilteevan 'there
were never any regulations or rules about days on which
a grave could be dug'.[144] Similarly in the Shannon area of
west Longford:

When a person dies a few friends or neighbours of the deceased dig the grave on the morning of the burial, because a grave must not be left open overnight. There is no special day on which a grave must not be dug, nor any belief that a woman should not point out the site of a grave.[145]

A superstition in north-east Galway, which Michael Coughlan referred to was: 'That a man should not dig more than two graves in the one year'. He asked a man on one occasion to help in the digging of a grave, and the man said that he had already dug two graves and that it would not be right to dig a third.[146] In earlier times when burials took place in churchyards rather than in separate cemetries, burials did not take place on the north side. Graves were usually orientated in an east west direction but this rule was not always adhered to. The grave was usually five feet in depth, six and a half feet long or seven feet and two feet wide. John Stroker, of Kilteevan, County Roscommon, who had a good reputation as a gravedigger described how a grave was made:

> First thing to do is to take off the sods. These are cut off first and heaped up beside the grave. When the grave is filled in these sods are placed back again. The centre of the grave should be opened first, by digging the centre of the grave you can make it neat and nice, but if you open the grave the full width, you'll have to make it too wide if you're to have it neatly done.[147]

In Longford care was taken when removing the sod from the top of the grave to keep it in one piece to be used in covering the grave later:

> The green sod of the grave is nicked all round first with a spade and then this green sod is rolled up like a mat and put at the head of the grave, till the grave is filled in. When the earth is taken out of the grave it is heaped up on the south side of the grave.[148]

In all of the accounts the gravediggers took care in storing and re-interring bones that were removed, and a sense of respect for the dead and compassion for the family of the deceased was conveyed. When they had finished digging the grave it was customary to drink the whiskey that had been provided by the family of the deceased.

Michael Coughlan described making a grave, in the early 1960s, when the curate in the Parish of Killeroran, north-east Galway, died. After the grave was dug a mixture of concrete was made up to form a floor, then they built the sides of the grave with concrete blocks (4"x9"), to a height of about three feet. The grave was then left for the cement to harden for a few hours. Later they lined the remainder of the grave, from the top of the concrete walls, with planks the required length and breadth of the grave, respectively. The grave was then lined with moss, so that looking at it you could see only a lining of moss.[149] A somewhat similar procedure was carried out in making a grave for a schoolteacher in Ballintubber in the 1967. The grave was lined with concrete blocks up to a height of about four feet and these were then covered with timber planks across the full length of the grave.[150] In the folklore investigated there were only two references to graves being lined in this manner. 'The Stroker family of Kilteevan, had a grave that was lined with brick, but they took the bricks out of it'.[151] As a rule graves of Catholics were not lined with anything; graves of Protestants were sometimes lined with moss or other evergreens.

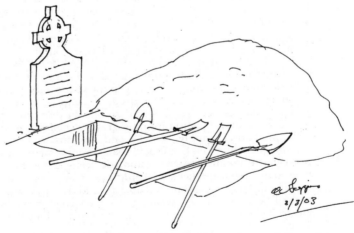

Drawing by Albert Siggins of crossed spades and shovels

In all of the earlier folklore accounts the spade and shovel used for digging and removing earth, were placed over the open grave to form a cross, in order according to traditional belief, to keep evil spirits from entering the grave. 'The spade and shovel are always placed cross wise over the open grave, and the reason for doing so, is to prevent any evil spirit from entering the grave, before the coffin is put into it'.[152] An explanation for the custom is found in folklore in the Geevagh area of southeast Sligo: When St. Patrick was working in Tír Amhalghaidh, County Mayo, he had a servant named Domhnall. One of his duties was to collect firewood and one day when he had his bundle of firewood collected he was unable to lift it as it was fastened to the ground. He looked round and saw a little fairy man watching him; the fairy offered to lift the bundle if the boy in return did him a small favour. The boy consented and the fairy then told him what he required done:

"Tomorrow morning, when you are serving Mass for Patrick, ask him, precisely at the elevation of the Host, what is going to happen to the *Sidh* or fairy-folk on the Last Day". The boy promised to do so and at the precise moment the following morning, he asked the saint as directed. "They'll all be lost!" replied Patrick. When Mass was over Patrick asked him why he had asked him that question during Mass and Domhnall explained that he had promised a fairy man to do so. "O wretched creature!" exclaimed Patrick, "when you tell them my answer they'll tear you limb from limb". He advised him to go to the trysting place in the wood, and there to dig his grave, good and deep, and then to lie down in it, having first arranged the spade and shovel, or whatever weapons were then used, in the form of a cross over the open grave. The boy did so and in due time the fairy appeared and peered into the grave. When Domhnall told him Patrick's reply, shrieks and screams as from a million fairies burst on Domhnall's ears. Innumerable fairies in vengeful mood appeared round the open grave, but to Domhnall's intense relief they could not enter the grave or touch him. The story got noised abroad, and thus the people learned how the crossed weapons over an open grave are able to keep out spirits, and so it has been perpetuated ever since.[153]

As Christiansen points out, in Irish oral tradition, the fairies are supposed to be the Fallen Angels or their descendants and speculation arose about their ultimate fate.

> The story is that a man, or sometimes a woman, met a crowd of the other race and was charged with the discovery of their final fate by asking a saint, e.g. St. Patrick, or a priest, during the elevation of the host, as it was then impossible to tell a lie. In both cases the answer was that there was no hope, since they had no drop of human blood in their veins, not even as much as to enable them to sign their names.[154]

This legend has been recorded in widely separated parts of the country and according to Mac Néill, is said 'to be the origin of the crossed spade and shovel at burials'.[155] In folklore in south Roscommon an explanation for the 'Fallen Angels' is found and in this account they are actually saved on the Day of Judgement:

> Lucifer was the head angel in Heaven. And Lucifer got so proud that he should have as much power in the maintenance of Heaven as God Himself. So God made Hell and He cast Lucifer down with the rebellious angels. There were some angels that didn't ayther condemn Lucifer or coincide. They kept dumb, He cast them out. And they were fallin' from Heaven and God said: "As they are, let them be." And some were hangin' out of Heaven, and some were half way between earth and Heaven. Some were on the ground and these on the ground are what we call fairies. They'll be here until the Day of Judgement. And then they'll be brought back to Heaven.[156]

An account of the origin of the fairies which the narrator from Derrycassin, County Longford, had heard from older people is similar but there is no reference to their fate on the last day:

> When the war was in Heaven between the Fallen Angels and the Good Angels, the Fallen Angels were all fallin' from Heaven and Michael the Archangel asked Almighty God, "Lord", he says, "will you lay waste the Heavens"? And God said, "as they are, let them be", and the angels that were all fallin' stayed where they were at that time. Some were in the air and they stopped there. Some were on earth and they stopped on earth and the angels that stopped on earth are the fairies.[157]

The custom of forming a cross over the grave with the spade and shovel continued in many areas until the late twentieth century. It is still practised in Fuerty graveyard, west of Roscommon town, according to

Albert Siggins: 'Spades and shovels are laid in a cross shape after the grave has been dug and are left like this overnight awaiting the burial the following day'.[158] According to gravediggers in Cam, Rahara and Knockcroghery, where there are old graveyards, it is still customary to place the spade and shovel across the open grave to form a cross.[159]

Graveyard

Ritual was in evidence when the corpse reached the graveyard as it was an important threshold where certain rites were enacted. 'The same four that brings the coffin from the house to the street, they have to carry the coffin again into the Churchyard'.[160] At some older graveyards there were coffin rests, and many of them are still in evidence in Galway and Mayo in particular. One particular coffin rest in Kiltullagh, east Galway, is at the crossroads nearest the graveyard.

Coffin rest at Kiltullagh

Coffin rest at Killaan

Many of the coffin rests served originally as the entrance to the graveyard, such as that at Killaan, County Galway, and the coffin was rested there for a short period before it was lifted by the four specially chosen by name to carry the remains to the grave. The grave was never approached directly:

> Sul a cuirtear an corp ins an uaigh tugtar timpeall na roilige ar an taobh istigh den mballa é trí uaire – Gnás é seo atá i gceanntar in iarthar Mhuigheó.

> [Before the body is put in the grave it is taken round the graveyard inside the wall three times – This is a custom in west Mayo].[161]

The practice on reaching the graveyard in the parish of Newtown Cashel, Longford was: 'A complete circle of the graveyard in an anti-clockwise direction was made and then they approached the grave'.[162] In the parish of Killeroran, Galway the following was observed:

> In the churchyard of Killyan [Killaan], some funerals approach and there is a gate into the churchyard on the road they come, but they don't use the near gate, but circle the churchyard and enter it on the opposite side from which they approached it. Then they walk around the inside of the churchyard and approach the grave by a circuitous route.[163]

In all the folklore studied the coffin was brought by a circuitous route because people did not like to seem to be in a hurry to bury the deceased. Fear of the dead and a desire to confuse evil spirits which might be in attendance was another reason.

The only time when a funeral made undue haste into the graveyard was when it met another funeral. 'One funeral would try to be before the other as they used to say that the last one in had to mind the gate until the next funeral came'.[164] This practice was recorded throughout the midlands and the belief was similar in all accounts:

> If there were two funerals comin' to the graveyard, there'd be a race, with the bearers, in order to be the first to the graveyard. They believed that the last one buried would have to be caretaker of the churchyard until the next one would be buried.[165]

Some narrators referred to an actual fight taking place because people were so superstitious about being last in:

> When two arrived at the churchyard together, to be buried, the last man in the churchyard would have to guard it. Hence the friends of the dead people fought for first place into the graveyard, so that their friend would not have to guard it.[166]

Stones through which the coffin was carried in Moyne churchyard

The coffin was never left down on the ground on the funeral route and this practice was followed when it reached the graveyard, unless there was some special place which had significance in folk memory. 'The coffin had to be placed on the newly dug clay that was taken from the grave when it arrived at the graveyard'.[167] At Cloonkeenkerrill, at present coffins are rested on a recently constructed coffin rest in the graveyard. 'Prior to the erection of this monument coffins were placed on the ground at this spot which is said to mark St. Kerrill's grave'.[168]

When the priest attended the burial he blessed the grave with holy water before the coffin was lowered into it. In earlier times before ropes were used to lower the coffin, the grave was made long enough so that two men had room to stand in the grave at each end. 'The coffin had to be lowered into the grave feet first, at about an angle of sixty or more; otherwise it couldn't be done at all'.[169] It was recorded in 1938 in northwest Roscommon that when the priest was there for the burial: 'He takes the shovel with which the grave was made, and throws three shovelfuls of clay in on the coffin, saying at the same time. *Memento etc*'.[170] In the Lough Ree area of County Longford the custom was similar, 'the priest at a burial puts in three shovels of blessed clay into the grave, on top of the coffin'.[171] In the nineteenth century France also, 'the priest would throw a piece of earth on the coffin, and then the mourners, starting with the family, would pass by and sprinkle it with holy water one last time'.[172]

It was customary for all to help in filling in the grave after the first three shovelfuls of earth had been put in. Anything that had been removed from the grave during digging was placed on top of the new coffin or at its foot:

> The owner of the corpse takes the bones off the shovel as the grave diggers lift them and places them down at the foot of the grave and then puts them in with the coffin, when it is being buried. (James Delaney note: the owner here would imply the head of the house, from which the person was being buried).[173]

In Britain commonly observed customs included 'the carrying by mourners of rosemary or other evergreens, which were dropped into the grave after the coffin'.[174] In

Ballymoe it was recorded that Protestants graves 'are lined with moss and flowers are strewn over the coffin as it is lowered into the grave'.[175] The bones, remains of other coffins, and sometimes the bottle which held the holy water were placed in the graves of Catholics according to folklore records. The practice of strewing flowers into the grave is a recent custom at Catholic funerals.

The method of covering the grave was similar in most of the material investigated but in some areas there were slight variations. In some accounts, particularly from older narrators, it was customary to cover the grave with a scraw from some other place or with sods taken from the grave when digging it. In Kiltoom a particular custom was observed which John Kenny had heard from his grandfather:

> They used to cut a scraw in Strevins's field, outside the graveyard, to cover the grave. The scraw would be three feet wide and seven feet long. It would be rolled on a round piece of stick, and six men carried it into the graveyard. The scraw was spread over the grave, when it was filled in. That custom is done away with now, since the old graveyard was shut down.[176]

In Dysart graveyard they also went into the next field to get a scraw to cover the grave; a custom that was practised in most of the older graveyards in this area.

> In Rahara you have to bring a scraw off your own land, if you haven't a friend near the graveyard that would give you one. But they always put a green scraw over the grave, when it is filled in. It was the same in Cam graveyard, in the original graveyard, but not now.[177]

Another example of the taking of sods from elsewhere other than the grave is provided from Kilteevan.

> The sods for the grave were always got in another field, long ago. The sods were about sixteen in number and they were about the length of the head of the spade and about twice the breadth. Whatever number of sods were needed for the grave, it was the custom to cut three more over and above the number required. These three sods were left on the wall of the graveyard.[178]

As was mentioned earlier clay pipes were left for people to help themselves on the day of the funeral and they were also brought to the graveyard. 'A man with a skib of pipes would be at the funeral also, and he would be giving out pipes and tobacco to the people at the funeral, as they went along'.[179] Smoking, as a rite of incorporation was important, and thus at the graveside before the final separation, pipes were smoked in honour of the deceased. Angela Partridge refers to folklore collected in northwest Mayo (CBÉ 714:280-3) which explains *'gurb í an Mhaighdean Mhuire an chéad duine a chaith tobac ar thórramh nuair a chaith sí píopa ag bun na Croise'.* [that the Blessed Virgin was the first person to smoke tobacco at a funeral when she smoked a pipe at the foot of the Cross].[180] The belief that the Blessed Virgin smoked at the tomb of Our Lord is substantiated in folklore collected in Longford in the mid 1950s. 'The Blessed Virgin was weepin' beside the tomb and she said, "if we had pipes and tobacco it'd aise our minds," and with that pipes and tobacco appeared on the tombstone'.[181] The pipes that were left over were left on the grave as is evidenced in the quantities of clay pipes that have been found buried beside headstones. 'Any pipes that were left over after the funeral, were left on the grave, with the bearer'.[182]

The following custom was observed in Kilmovee, east Mayo, according to the narrator who heard it from his grandfather:

> Dá bhfaghadh fear nó bean óg bás a mbeadh clann in a ndiaidh, nuair a chuirfí síos ins an uaigh iad dá mbeadh na páistí sáthach sean le bheith ag an uaigh, nuair a bheadh an uaigh druidthe, bhéarfadh duine eicínt muinnteardhach gach páiste aca ar a 'd'turn treasna an uaigh agus ar fad an uaigh.

> [If a young man or woman died who had left a family behind them, when they were placed in the grave if the children were old enough to be at the grave, when the grave was closed, some relative would pass every one of the children in turn across the grave and down its length].[183]

A similar custom is found in folklore in east Galway when a young parent died:

> If a parent dies, they make the children cross the grave three times, to lessen the children's sorrow. The children stand at either side of the grave and catch hands across the grave and then step or jump across, one exchanging sides with the other. This is done three times.[184]

A slight variation of this custom is found in superstitions concerning death:

> Nuair atá an uaigh dúnta is cóir do na gaoltaibh is goire do'n té a cuireadh siubhal treasna na huaighe trí uaire, agus má déantar sin ní bheidh an brón ná an cúmha mór orra.

> [When the grave is closed the nearest relatives of the person who was buried should walk across the grave three times and if that is done their grief will not be as great].[185]

The latter practice was also known in traditional belief in southeast Sligo as a means of assuaging grief: 'If someone, the next of kin, was very grieved, just when the grave is finished, someone would take them by the hand, and walk them over the grave three times and they'd bless themselves'.[186] Usually children did not attend the burial in earlier times, nor did pregnant women. Older people considered that 'it wasn't right for a pregnant woman to enter a graveyard', according to folklore in east Galway.[187] When the priest was present, as was usually the case in the Diocese of Elphin, as soon as the grave was filled in he recited a decade of the Rosary. People usually visited family graves when the burial was over, according to material recorded in Ballymoe, and in other areas it was the custom also.

> Many people take the advantage of a funeral in the graveyard to pray over the graves of their deceased friends. As it is an old superstitious belief that it is unlucky to enter a graveyard except with a funeral – if you do you will soon die.[188]

Once the funeral was over, it was acceptable for the mourners to take a short cut home, through the fields or by a direct route. An older narrator, Peter Kilmartin, of Endrim, County Offaly, remembered seeing ten or fifteen horsemen trotting home in formation from funerals:

> It was a lovely sight to see them all goin' up and down. They'd all wheel for home, then, two be two along the road. They all kept together at a good trot. Ye wouldn't be allowed to gallop. But they'd go at a good trot, every man goin' up and down in the saddle and it was the grandest sight ever you seen.[189]

People returned home when the funeral was over and any food, drink or tobacco that was left over was shared out among their neighbours. The clothes of the deceased were given to the poor or were kept. The period of mourning observed by the family usually depended on their relationship to the deceased. As van Gennep points out:

> During mourning, the living mourners and the deceased constitute a special group, situated between the world of the living and the world of the dead, and how soon living individuals leave that group depends on the closeness of their relationship with the dead person.[190]

The immediate family did not attend any dances, sporting events or any other form of entertainment for a period of six to twelve months, depending on the age of the deceased. 'For an old person usually it lasts for six months. For a young person it lasts for twelve, for a very young person, it may only last a month'.[191] The family usually dressed in dark clothing, particularly widows, to denote that they were in mourning. In 1938, it was recorded 'people nowadays dress in black during the period of mourning, sometimes they wear grey clothes, with a black band or diamond shaped piece of crepe on the sleeve'.[192]

Cures and Practices associated with the Corpse following Death/Burial

Despite the view that death was feared and people felt threatened by it there was also evidence of a positive element associated with death. As Wilson points out: 'Since such power emanated from the dead, their remains and anything in contact with them had power by association'.[193] Cures associated with candles and snuff used when the person was dying and at the wake have already been referred to. In Ireland the belief that the hand of the corpse had curative properties was widely held: *'Tá leigheas i láimh an mharbháin'.i. Leigheasfar lot nó anshóg má cuimiltear lámh duine mhairbh dó'.* [There's a cure in the hand of a dead person i.e. a wound or discomfort can be cured if it is rubbed with the hand of a dead person].[194] References were made in the folklore accounts to cures associated with the hand of the corpse by some of the older narrators, thus it was believed that the hand of a dead woman had a cure:

I heard of a cure in the corpse. I saw a man got something on his jaw, some kind of a lump. He was discussin' this lump he had on his jaw and he said he got a dead woman's hand and rubbed it off it and it cured the lump.[195]

It was believed that it could also cure toothache: 'If you take the hand of a corpse and rub it on your face, if you had toothache, it would cure the toothache'.[196] A cure for toothache which Wood-Martin referred to was 'to drink water from a human skull'. In reference to a cure for epilepsy he quotes Grose, who was shown a skull in the graveyard of Clonthuskert, east Roscommon, "in which milk was boiled and given to a man afflicted with epilepsy". A well-known cure for this disorder according to Wood-Martin was 'to take nine pieces from the cranium of a dead man, grind them quite fine and dissolve them in a decoction of wall-rue'. He adds that the skull of Carolan was thus utilized by the peasantry.[197] Carolan, a composer harpist, is buried in Kilronan churchyard in north Roscommon, and according to local tradition, his skull, which was placed in a niche in the wall of the church, had cures associated with it. [198]

Turlough O'Carolan's Grave, Kilronan

Another instance of the hand of the corpse being used to effect a positive outcome was in its employment to increase butter output. The practice of using a dead hand to steal the neighbour's butter was recorded throughout the midlands. In Lissduff, County Offaly, the narrator had heard the following: 'They used to get a dead hand from the graveyard in aul' times to make up the butter with it. That's how they used to take the butter from the neighbours in aul' times'.[199] In Rooskey, County Roscommon, the narrator had heard from her mother about a neighbour who had a dead hand:

> She had this dead hand and when she'd churn, she'd take out the dead hand. And the neighbours used to be wonderin' where she got all the butter.and she goin' into the butter market every week in Longford with her rowl of butter. But a poor woman that was lodgin' the night with her, tould on her. The poor woman was lyin' down and the other lassie thought she was asleep. She saw her takin' a white cloth out of the cupboard and the hand was wrapped in the white cloth. And she took the hand and put it in the churn and she was sayin': "gather far and near, gather far and near, gather far and near". So me mother tould the priest what the travellin' woman tould her and the priest made the aul' lassie quit takin' butter'.[200]

In Kilmovee, east Mayo, a similar practice was recorded:

> 'Bhí bean ann fadó sa paróiste seo agus bhíodh sí ábalta an t-im a ghoid óna cuid comharsan. Bhí lámh fear marbh aici'.

> [There was a woman long ago in this parish and she was able to steal the butter from her neighbours. She had a dead man's hand].[201]

In Riverstown, County Sligo, the narrator heard that: 'A witch used turn herself into a cat and would need a dead hand to take the butter off the people'.[202] All of the above cures and customs were recorded as having been practised in earlier times and do not seem to have been observed in the twentieth century.

Changes in Burial Practice
Most of the customs began to change after it became obligatory to bring the corpse to the church the night before the burial in the first quarter of the twentieth century. Bearers had ceased to be used at this time; they were replaced by hearses. Bells were rung to announce

the arrival of the funeral procession and continued to ring while the coffin was being carried into the church. William Talbot sums it up thus:

> The first bell rings a half hour before the funeral. Then the second bell goes a short time after that. The third bell is called the offerin' bell. And when that goes everyone goes into the chapel to pay their offerin's. You have no business goin' to a funeral without your half-crown. The fourth bell goes when the funeral is movin' off from the door of the church.[203]

Although we associate bell ringing with religious ceremonies, Sharper Knowlson points out that originally 'the underlying idea was two-fold: to call the living Christian to prayer, and to scare the fiends who are waiting to pounce on a departing soul'.[204] A Requiem or Low Mass was said for the deceased on the morning of the funeral; sometimes the Requiem Mass took place a month later. The funeral usually took place in the early afternoon following Mass and bells were again rung to announce the removal of the remains from the church, as the former narrator pointed out.

Although customs changed as the twentieth century progressed some were still observed. When burial took place in the churchyard, the coffin was carried feet foremost, by four men, usually relatives of the deceased, to the grave. Otherwise a hearse was used to transport the coffin to the graveyard, if it was a distance away, but four people still carried the coffin into graveyard. The priest met the funeral at the graveyard, thus the various customs which had been part of funerary tradition began to die out. One custom which altered little was the digging of the grave but, whereas neighbours and relatives were involved previously, later on there were special gravediggers. Since the 1970s it has been customary to leave the filling in of the grave until the mourners have departed. Wreaths and flowers have replaced the green sods or scraws which were mandatory in the nineteenth and the first half of the twentieth century. Gradually the funeral changed from a social to a religious event and with the passage of time the older traditions were practically forgotten.

Whereas in the past people generally died at home, by the middle of the twentieth century, the place of death had shifted to the hospital. As Ariès has shown this transfer has had profound consequences. Life is prolonged with the aid of medicines and though the doctor cannot eliminate death, he can control its duration.[205] Death which had been public became less visible and private and the larger community and often the family were no longer involved. Even when death took place at home it became clinical and controlled and old traditions became obsolete. If one looks at the statistics for Ireland it is clear that change in burial customs was inevitable: 'In 1949, 65% of deaths occurred at home, while only 22% occurred there in 1998. This shows the greater availability and utilization of institutional care'.[206] But as Kübler-Ross points out: 'Death is still a fearful happening, and the fear of death is a universal fear even if we think we have mastered it on many levels'.[207]

Murry headstone, Killinvoy

Lord have mercy on
the soul of Martin Murry
who depd. this life Feb
the 2nd 1814 aged 60yrs also
his son John Murry who
depd this life May 11th 1812 aged 24 yrs erecd by his
Sons Bernard & Mikl
[remainder unclear]

deciphered by Jim Ganly

Notes

1   R. Grainger, *The Social Symbolism of Grief and Mourning*, London 1998, 128.
2   Mary Douglas, *Purity and Danger: An analysis of the concepts of pollution and taboo*, London 1979, 96.
3   IFC 1550:169, collected by James Delaney from Patrick Mc Donnell, Caltra, Co. Roscommon, 1959.
4   IFC 1551:390-1, collected by James Delaney from John Gately (Senior), Castletown, Curraghboy, Co. Roscommon, Feb. 1960.
5   IFC 1526:230, collected by James Delaney from Michael Gilligan, Cornageer, Cam, Co. Roscommon, March 1959.
6   IFC 1550:213, collected by James Delaney from John Noone, Kilclough, Toomard, Co. Galway, August, 1959.
7   1771:346, collected by James Delaney from Mrs. Allen, Williamstown, Mount Temple, Co. Westmeath, 1968.
8   IFC 1677:120-1, collected by James Delaney from William Talbot, Kilcormac, Co. Offaly, 1963.
9   IFC 1507:78, collected by James Delaney from James Milton, Bohy, Gortlettera, Co. Leitrim, July 1958.
10 IFC 1575:141, collected by James Delaney from John Dunning, Clonown, Co. Roscommon, 1961.
11 IFC 1487:76, collected by James Delaney from James Farrell, Furze, Lagan, Co. Longford, Oct. 1957.
12 IFC 1781:240, collected by James Delaney from William Maxwell, Dorrary, Drumlyon, Co. Roscommon, 1970.
13 IFC 1640:308, collected by James Delaney from William Talbot, Kilcormac, Co. Offaly, Nov.1963.
14 1771:24, collected by James Delaney from James Flynn, Shurock, Mount Temple, Co. Westmeath, Aug. 1967.
15 IFC 1550:284, collected by James Delaney from Michael Coughlan, Closhatoher, Co. Galway, Sept. 1958.
16 IFC 1639:235, collected by James Delaney from John Kenny, Newpark, Kiltoom, Co. Roscommon, 1963.
17 IFC 1550:236, Collected by James Delaney from Ellen Hogan, Coolderry, Four Roads, Co. Roscommon, Sept. 1958.
18 IFC 1507:432, collected by James Delaney from James Grady, Rinnegan, St. John's, Co. Roscommon, Nov. 1958.
19 T. Ó hAilín, 'Caointe agus Caointeoirí', *Feasta* Feabhra 1971, 5-9; 7.
20 IFC 1781:422, collected by James Delaney from John Kenny, Newtown, Kiltoom, Co. Roscommon, Jan. 1970.
21 IFC 1771:36, collected by James Delaney from Peter Kilmartin, Endrim, Co. Offaly, March 1967.
22 IFC 1205:591, collected by Ciarán Bairéad from John Rabbitte, Lackagh, Co. Galway, Oct. 1951.
23 IFC 549:234, collected by Bríd Ní Ghamhnáin, Ballindoon, Co. Roscommon, 1938.
24 IFC 1550:288, collected by James Delaney from Michael Coughlan, Closhatoher, Co. Galway, Sept. 1958.

25 IFC 1487:74, collected by James Delaney from James Farrell, Furze, Lagan, Co. Longford, Oct. 1957.

26 Gail Kligman, *The Wedding of the Dead: Ritual, Poetics, and Popular Culture in Transylvania*, Berkeley 1988, 171.

27 Kselman, *Death and the Afterlife in Modern France*, 52.

28 *Ibid.*, 53.

29 IFC 1782:89, collected by Michael Murphy from Mrs. Meehan, Sooey, Co. Sligo, March 1970.

30 IFC 1782:361, collected by Michael Murphy from John Currid, Shrananagh, Sooey, Co. Sligo, March 1970.

31 IFC 552:324, collected by Kathleen Hurley at Ballymoe, Co. Galway, 1938.

32 *Ibid.*, 325

33 Lysaght, 'Caoineadh ós Cionn Coirp: The Lament for the Dead in Ireland', 72.

34 IFC 1506:154 collected by James Delaney from John Naughton, Kilteevan, Co. Roscommon, 1958.

35 IFC 549:320, collected by Bríd Ní Ghamhnáin at Ballindoon, Co. Roscommon, 1938.

36 Richardson, 'Death's Door', 95.

37 *Ibid.*, 95.

38 Van Gennep, *Rites of Passage*, 20-1.

39 Kligman, *The Wedding of the Dead*, 193.

40 Feilberg, 'The Corpse-Door: A Danish Survival', 366.

41 *Ibid.*, 368.

42 IFC 1575:556, collected by James Delaney from Mrs Theresa Feeney and Patrick Feeney, Tully, Co. Galway, April 1962.

43 IFC 1575: 512, collected by James Delaney from Kieran Mc Manus, Nure Co. Roscommon, Feb. 1962.

44 Feilberg, 'The Corpse-Door: A Danish Survival', 364.

45 IFC 1487:76-7, collected by James Delaney from James Farrell, Furze, Lagan, Co. Longford, Oct. 1957.

46 IFC 1575:512, collected by James Delaney from Kieran Mc Manus, Nure, Co. Roscommon, Feb. 1962.

47 IFC 1550:169, collected by James Delaney from Patrick Mac Donnell, Caltra, Co. Roscommon, 1958.

48 Richardson, 'Death's Door', 95.

49 IFC 1551:391, collected by James Delaney from John Gately, Castletown, Curraghboy, Co. Roscommon, Feb 1960.

50 IFC 1506:547, collected by James Delaney from Mrs. Kate Ward, Corra More, Athleague, Co. Roscommon, June 1958.

51 IFC 552:327, collected by Bríd Ní Ghamhnáin at Ballindoon, Boyle, Co. Roscommon, 1938.

52 IFC 1575:449, collected by James Delaney from James Flynn, Clonown, Co. Roscommon, Jan. 1962.

53 IFC 1506:547-8, collected by James Delaney from Mrs. Kate Ward, Corramore, Athleague, Co. Roscommon, June 1958.

54 IFC 1399:594, collected by James Delaney from James Farrell, Inchcleraun, Lough Ree, Co. Longford, 1955.

[55] IFC 1575:512, collected by James Delaney from Kieran Mc Manus, Nure, Co. Roscommon, Feb. 1962.

[56] H. Rice, *Thanks for the Memory*, Athlone 1975, 71.

[57] IFC 1399:580-1, collected by James Delaney from James Farrell, Inchcleraun, Co. Longford, Aug. 1955.

[58] *Ibid.*, 582.

[59] IFC 1480:144, collected by James Delaney from Kate Flood, Cranally, Co. Longford, Dec.1956.

[60] IFC 1480;6, collected by James Delaney from Patrick Hetherton, Derreenavoggy, Co. Longford, Nov. 1956.

[61] IFC 1399:595, collected by James Delaney from James Farrell, Inchcleraun, Co. Longford, Aug. 1955.

[62] IFC 1575:510-3, collected by James Delaney from Kieran Mc Manus, Nure, Co. Roscommon, Feb. 1962.

[63] IFC 1677:348, collected by James Delaney from John Connaughton, Lisduff, Tissarain, Co. Offaly, Sept. 1963.

[64] IFC 1507:9, collected by James Delaney from Joseph Hanley, Clooneigh, Four Roads, Co. Roscommon, May, 1958.

[65] IFC 1639:225, collected by James Delaney from John Lennon, Kilmaccormac, Drum, Co. Roscommon, Nov. 1962.

[66] IFC 1796:312, collected by James Delaney from William Egan, Clonfanlough, Co. Offaly, Jan. 1970.

[67] IFC 1536:244, collected by James Delaney, from Michael Gilligan, Cornageer, Curraghboy, Co. Roscommon, March 1959.

[68] IFC 1506:547, collected by James Delaney from Mrs. Kate Ward, Corra More, Athleague, Co. Roscommon, June 1958.

[69] IFC 1551:3, collected by James Delaney from Michael Coughlan, Closhatoher, Co. Galway, Oct. 1959.

[70] IFC 1575: 410, collected by James Delaney from Kieran Mc Manus, Nure, Drum, Co. Roscommon, Feb. 1962.

[71] IFC 1639:341, collected by James Delaney from John Devery, Lecarrow, Clonmacnoise, Co. Offaly, Jan. 1963.

[72] *Ibid.*, 343.

[73] Weld, *A Survey of the County of Roscommon*, 563.

[74] IFC 1771:25, collected by James Delaney from James Flynn, Shurock, Co. Westmeath, Aug. 1967.

[75] IFC 1834:203, collected by James Delaney from John Kenny, Newtown, Kiltoom, Co. Roscommon, 1973.

[76] 1639:225, collected by James Delaney from John Lennon, Kilmaccormac, Co. Roscommon, Nov. 1962.

[77] IFC 1550: 295, collected by James Delaney from Michael Coughlan, Closhatoher, Co. Galway, Sept. 1958.

[78] IFC 1640:310, collected by James Delaney from William Talbot, Kilcormac, Co. Offaly, Nov. 1963.

[79] IFC 552:352, collected by Bríd Ní Ghamhnáin at Ballindoon, Co. Roscommon, 1938.

[80] IFC 1506:548-10, collected by James Delaney from Mrs. Kate Ward, Corra More, Athleague, Co. Roscommon, June 1958.

81   IFC 1550:296, collected by James Delaney from Michael Coughlan, Closhatoher, Co. Galway, Sept. 1958.
82   Anon., 'Weddings and Wakes', *The Dublin University Magazine*, Dublin 1876, 295.
83   IFC 1573:13-4, collected by James Delaney from John Gately, Castletown, Curraghboy, Co. Roscommon, Feb. 1960.
84   IFC 1550:190, collected by James Delaney from Martin Nolan, Liosavruggy, Ballygar, Co. Galway, 1959.
85   *Ibid.*, 191.
86   IFC 1573:14, collected by James Delaney from John Gately (Senior), Castletown, Curraghboy, Co. Roscommon, Feb. 1960.
87   IFC 1550:285, collected by James Delaney from Michael Coughlan, Closhatoher, Co. Galway, Sept. 1958.
88   IFC 1205:12, collected by Ciarán Bairéad from Andy Mc. Donagh, Gort a' tSléibhe, Baile Cláir na Gaillimhe, 1951.
89   IFC 1550:34, collected by James Delaney from John Flanagan, Mount Talbot, Co. Roscommon, June 1959.
90   Wood-Martin, *Traces of the Elder Faiths of Ireland*, 325.
91   IFC 1640:310, collected by James Delaney from William Talbot, Kilcormac, Co. Offaly, Oct. 1963.
92   IFC 1575:410, collected from Kieran Mc Manus, Nure, Co. Roscommon, Jan. 1962.
93   IFC 1506:549, collected by James Delaney from Mrs. Kate Ward, Corra More, Athleague, Co. Roscommon, June 1958.
94   IFC 1550:34, collected by James Delaney from John Flanagan, Mount Talbot, Co. Roscommon, June 1959.
95   IFC 1498:1, collected by Pádraig Mac Gréine from Mrs. Oney Power, Ballymahon, Co. Longford, July 1957.
96   Richardson, 'Death's Door', 96.
97   Evans, *Irish Folk Ways*, 293.
98   IFC 1506:548, collected by James Delaney from Mrs. Kate Ward, Corra More, Athleague, Co. Roscommon, June 1958.
99   IFC 552:326, collected by Kathleen Hurley at Ballymoe, Co. Galway, 1938.
100   IFC 1864:208, James Delaney, Kiltoom, Co. Roscommon, 1973.
101   IFC 1506:154, collected by James Delaney from John Naughton, Kilteevan, Co. Roscommon, Feb. 1958.
102   IFC 1677:560-1, collected by James Delaney from Patrick Johnson, Ballinlassie, Co. Westmeath, Sept. 1964.
103   IFC 1639:224, collected from John Lennon, Kilmaccormac, Drum, Co. Roscommon, Nov. 1962.
104   Lysaght, 'Caoineadh os Cionn Coirp: The Lament for the Dead in Ireland', 75.
105   Information received from Mary O'Connell. Tonrevagh, Castlerea, Co. Roscommon, May 2003.
106   IFC 1639:380-1, collected by James Delaney from Michael Shanny, Kilcashel, Moor, Co. Roscommon, 1963.
107   IFC 1575:408, collected by James Delaney from Kieran Mc Manus, Nure, Co. Roscommon, Feb. 1962.

[108] Edward Egan, Brochure by Drum Heritage Group, Co. Roscommon, April 2003.

[109] IFC 1639:224, collected by James Delaney from John Lennon, Kilmaccormac, Co. Roscommon. Nov. 1962.

[110] P. Tohall, 'The Diamond Fight of 1795 and the Resultant Expulsions', Seanchas Ardmhacha 1 Armagh (1958), 16-50.

[111] Ibid., 17-32.

[112] P. Harbison, Pilgrimage in Ireland, London 1991, 144.

[113] IFC1677:278, collected by James Delaney from Thomas Daly, Clooneyderg, Ballinahown, Co. Offaly, Oct. 1963.

[114] IFC 1771:326, footnote by James Delaney to account by Peter Kilmartin, Endrim, Co. Offaly, March 1967.

[115] IFC 1677:77, collected by James Delaney from John Connaughton, Lisduff, Co. Offaly, Sept. 1963.

[116] IFC 1639:380, collected by James Delaney from Michael Shanny, Kilcashel, Moor, Co. Roscommon, 1963.

[117] IFC 1639:341-2, collected by James Delaney from John Devery, Lecarrow, Co. Offaly, Jan. 1963.

[118] IFC 1575:509, collected by James Delaney from Kieran Mc Manus, Nure, Co. Roscommon, Feb. 1962.

[119] Ibid., 342.

[120] Máire Nic Néill, 'Wayside Death Cairns in Ireland', Béaloideas 16 (1946), 49-63; 59.

[121] IFC 653:192, collected by Philip Mac Aonghusa, Eslin N. S. Co. Leitrim, Sept. 1939.

[122] IFC 653:575-6, collected by Maureen Mullen from Lawrence Mullen, Aughrim, Co. Galway, March 1939.

[123] IFC 653:151-2, collected by Peadar Mac Giolla Coinnigh, Cloon, Co. Leitrim, Jan. 1939.

[124] IFC 653:454, collected by Micheál Ó Mainnín, Belclare, Co. Galway, from his neighbours, April 1939.

[125] IFC 653:520-40, collected by Kathleen Hurley, at Ballymoe, Co. Galway, 1939.

[126] Ibid., 548.

[127] Kselman, Death and the Afterlife in Modern France, 54.

[128] Margaret Stokes, 'Funeral Custom in Baronies of Bargy and Forth', J.R.S.A.I. 24 (1894), 380-5; 381.

[129] Ibid., 385.

[130] IFC 782:261, collected by P. J. O'Sullivan, Derrygorman, Aunascaul, Co. Kerry, 1941.

[131] Information received from Noel O'Neill, Castlebar, Co. Mayo, June 2008.

[132] IFC 1834:161, James Delaney.

[133] Cáit Ní Bhrádaigh, 'Folklore from Co. Longford', Béaloideas 6 (1936), 257-69; 261.

[134] Information received from Edward Egan, Drum Heritage Group, Aug. 2003.

[135] Information received from Albert Siggins, Fuerty Co. Roscommon, July 2003.

[136] Richardson, 'Death's Door: Thresholds and Boundaries in British Funeral Customs', 99.

[137] IFC 1399:596, collected by James Delaney from James Farrell, Inchcleraun, Lough Ree, Co. Longford, 1955.

[138] IFC 1507:432, collected by James Delaney from James Grady, Rinnagan, St. John's, Co. Roscommon, Nov. 1958.

[139] IFC 79:611; S. Mág Uidhir 'Pisreoga a Bhaineas leis an mBás', Béaloideas 3 (1932), 67-8; 67.

[140] IFC 1677:289, collected by James Delaney from Thomas Daly, Cloonyderg, Ballynahowan, Co. Offaly, Sept. 1963.

[141] IFC 1640:284, collected by James Delaney from John Connaughton, Lisduff, Co. Offaly, July 1963.

[142] IFC 1639:253, collected by James Delaney from Mrs. William Kenny, America, Moor, Co. Roscommon, Nov. 1962.

[143] Mannion Joseph, Saint Kerrill, Founder and Parton Saint of Cloonkeenkerrill, Commemorative Booklet, 2006,19.

[144] IFC 1506:479, collected by James Delaney from John Stroker, Kilteevan, Co. Roscommon, June 1958.

[145] IFC 1458:546-7, collected by James Delaney from James Fagan, Saint's Island, Co. Longford, Oct. 1958.

[146] IFC 1551:236, collected by James Delaney from Michael Coughlan, Closhatoher, Co. Galway, Jan. 1960.

[147] IFC 1506:480, collected by James Delaney from John Stroker, Kilteevan, Co. Roscommon, June 1958.480.

[148] IFC 1458:547, collected by James Delaney from James Fagan, Saint's Island, Co. Longford, Oct. 1958.

[149] IFC 1575:563, collected by James Delaney from Michael Coughlan, Closhatoher, Co Galway, April 1962.

[150] Information received from Gerry O'Brien, Ballintubber, Co. Roscommon, July 2003.

[151] IFC 1506: 483, collected by James Delaney from John Stroker, Kilteevan, Co. Roscommon, June 1958.

[152] IFC 549:333, collected by Bríd Ní Ghamhnain, at Ballindoon, Boyle, Co. Roscommon, 1938.

[153] É. Ó Muirgheasa, 'A Co. Sligo Tradition', Béaloideas 11 (1930), 138-9.

[154] Reidar Christiansen, 'Some Notes on the Fairies and the Fairy Faith', Béaloideas 39 (1975), 95-111; 96-8.

[155] Maire Mac Neill, The Festival of Lughnasa, 1, Dublin 1982, 397.

[156] IFC 1640:145, collected by James Delaney from Michael Shanny, Kilcashel, Co. Roscommon, 1963.

[157] IFC 1480:80, collected by James Delaney from James Rogers, Derrycassin, Co. Longford, Dec. 1956.

[158] Information received from Albert Siggins, Fuerty, Co. Roscommon, March 2003.

[159] Information received from Thomas Shaughnessy, Rahara, Co. Roscommon, August 2003.

[160] IFC 1575: 511, collected by James Delaney from Kieran Mc Manus, Nure, Co. Roscommon Feb. 1962.

[161] IFC 79:612, 'Pisreóga a haineas leis an mBás'.
[162] IFC 1399:596, collected by James Delaney from James Farrell, Inchcleraun, Lough Ree, Co. Longford, 1955.
[163] IFC 1550:295-6, collected by James Delaney from Michael Coughlan, Closhatoher, Co. Galway,Sept. 1959.
[164] IFC 1781:235, collected by James Delaney from William Maxwell, Doorary, Cootehall, Co. Roscommon, May 1970.
[165] IFC 1677:289, collected by James Delaney from Thomas Daly, Cloonyderg, Co. Offaly, Sept. 1963.
[166] IFC 1506:550-1, collected by James Delaney from Mrs. Kate Ward, Corramore, Athleague, Co. Roscommon, June 1958.
[167] IFC 1550:287, collected by James Delaney from Michael Coughlan, Closhatoher, Co. Galway, Sept. 1959.
[168] Mannion, J. The life, legends and legacy of Saint Kerrill: a fifth century East Galway evangelist, Temple Printing Co. Ltd. Athlone, 2004, 99.
[169] IFC 1506:483, collected by James Delaney from John Stroker, Kilteevan, Co. Roscommon, June 1958.
[170] IFC 549: 351, collected by Bríd Ní Ghamhnáin, at Ballindoon, Boyle, Co. Roscommon. 1938.
[171] IFC 1458:548, collected by James Delaney from James Fagan, Saint's Island, Co. Longford, Oct. 1958.
[172] Kselman, Death and the Afterlife in Modern France, 54.
[173] IFC 1399:596, collected by James Delaney from James Farrell, Inchcleraun, Co. Longford, 1955.
[174] Richardson, 'Death's Door', 100.
[175] IFC 552:316, collected by Kathleen Hurley at Ballymoe, Co. Galway, 1938.
[176] IFC 1639:237-8, collected by James Delaney from John Kenny, Newtown, Kiltoom, Co. Roscommon, 1963.
[177] IFC 1575:395-6, collected by James Delaney from John Gately, Castletown, Curraghboy, Co. Roscommon, 1960.
[178] IFC 1506:482-3, collected by James Delaney from John Stroker, Kilteevan, Co. Roscommon, June 1958.
[179] IFC 1550:33, collected by James Delaney from John Flanagan, Mount Talbot, Co. Roscommon, June 1959.
[180] Angela Partridge, Caoineadh na dTrí Muire, Baile Átha Cliath, 1983, 20.
[181] IFC 1457:6, collected by James Delaney from John Reilly, Drumhaldry, Dromard, Co. Longford, Feb. 1956.
[182] IFC 1550:33-4, collected by James Delaney from John Flanagan, Mount Talbot, Co. Roscommon, June 1959.
[183] IFC 194:55-7, collected by Pádraig Ó Ceannaigh from Pádraig Ó Reagáin, Cluain Fiachra, Béal Átha hAmhnais, Co. Mhaigh Eo, Bealtaine 1935.
[184] IFC 1550:288, collected by James Delaney from Michael Coughlan, Closhatoher, Co. Galway, Sept. 1958.
[185] S. Mág Uidhir, 'Pisreóga a Bhaineas leis an mBás', Béaloideas 3 (1932), 67-8; 67.

[186] IFC1782:89, collected by Michael J. Murphy, from Mrs. J. Meehan. Sooey, Co. Sligo,1970.

[187] IFC1550:286, collected by James Delaney from Michael Coughlan, Closhatoher, Co. Galway, Sept. 1959.

[188] IFC 552:314, collected by Kathleen Hurley at Ballymoe, Co. Galway, 1938.

[189] IFC 1771:34, collected by James Delaney from Peter Kilmartin, Endrim, Co. Offaly, March, 1968.

[190] Van Gennep, *The Rites of Passage*, 147.

[191] IFC 552:334, collected by Bríd Ní Ghamhnáin at Ballindoon, Co. Roscommon, 1938.

[192] *Ibid.*, 333-4.

[193] Wilson, *The Magical Universe*, 306.

[194] T. Ó Máille, eag., *Sean-fhocla Chonnacht*, 1, Baile Átha Cliath 1948, 62.

[195] IFC 1550:92, collected by James Delaney from John Flanagan, Mount Talbot, Co. Roscommon, 1959.

[196] IFC 1550:66, collected by James Delaney from Mrs. Hanley, Derraghmylan, Rooskey, Co. Roscommon, 1958.

[197] Wood-Martin, *Traces of the Elder Faiths of Ireland*, 296.

[198] *Ibid.*, 296.

[199] IFC 1640:288, collected by James Delaney from John Connaughton, Lissduff, Co. Offaly, July 1963.

[200] IFC 1550:65-6, collected by James Delaney from Mrs Mary Anne Hanley, Derraghmylan, Rooskey, Co. Roscommon, 1958.

[201] IFC 194:71-3, collected by Pádraig Ó Ceannaigh from Eoghan Ó Nualláin, Urlár, Béal Átha hÁmhnais, Co. Mhaigh Eo, 1935.

[202] IFC 1782: 414, collected by Michael Murphy from John Jackson, Lavally, Sooey, Co. Sligo, 1970.

[203] IFC 1640:306, collected by James Delaney from William Talbot, Kilcormac, Co. Offaly, Nov. 1963.

[204] Sharper Knowlson, *The Origins of Popular Superstitions and Customs*, 212.

[205] Ariès, *The Hour of Our Death*, 584-5.

[206] Mary Heanue, 'Matters of Life and Death', in *That was then, This is now: Change in Ireland, 1949-1999*, Dublin 2000, 29-44; 35.

[207] Elizabeth Kübler-Ross, *On Death and Dying*, New York 1997, 19.

Death is a major rite of passage, leading the individual from the known to the unknown, and as such it is accompanied by rituals which mark the deceased's departure from the world of the living. In traditional societies people fear death and they relied on established traditional customs to placate the deceased and ensure safe passage to the next world. In most traditional societies rites of passage, which van Gennep subdivides into rites of separation, transition rites, and rites of incorporation, were observed at the time of death, and during the wake and funeral. Folklore collected by part-time folklore collectors in the late 1930s and by the fulltime collector, James Delaney, from the late 1950s to late 1970s in the midlands, shows that death and burial were highly ritualized events. The rituals correspond to various stages of rites of passage as outlined by van Gennep and they are viewed as having helped people control their fear of death.

Birth, by which one comes into this world, and death by which one leaves it, are two major rites of passage in which women are directly involved; both physically and emotionally. The role of women in washing, laying out and lamenting the corpse was of paramount importance in ensuring successful separation of the dead person from the community. In Irish traditional society three women were involved in washing and laying out the corpse and according to one strand of folk tradition they symbolized the Three Marys at the foot of the cross and at the tomb of Christ. The rituals observed in the rites of separation also followed religious beliefs, most were home based and women played a leading role in them. Women watched over the corpse, they remained constantly by its side and if one moved away another took her place. Keening as a rite of separation was performed by women, very rarely were men involved, and it took place at key times during the liminal period when the deceased was in transition between this world and the next.

The caring role of women can be seen in the measures taken to protect the living and the dead, such as renewing the lighted candles so that the deceased was never left in darkness. People feared the dark and the candles were important in the rite of passage as they provided light for the deceased's journey and ensured successful transition. The ritual of saying the Rosary at the time of death, when the corpse was laid out, at midnight, and after the coffining, was important. By emphasizing the role of Our Lady at death its intonation attempted to ensure successful passing and incorporation into the next world. Our Lady lamenting her son is the archival type figure for all grievers in the Christian tradition and she was invoked at the key periods of lamentation. All present took part in the Rosary; it enabled the mourners to have an active role in helping the deceased to exit this world and helped secure successful incorporation.

Men were involved in the duties which took place outside the home for the most part. Generally three men went for the requisites for the wake and three men dug the grave, although a fourth might be present. They were in charge of the distribution of pipes, tobacco, and drink, which were an important part of the funerary rites aimed at ensuring successful separation. These rituals did not necessarily always take place in close proximity to the deceased but, as rites of social bonding, they helped people overcome their fear of death. The role of men was important during the period of transition from the familiar world of the home to that of the dead. Four men of the same name carried the coffin from the house and the same four carried it into the graveyard. The act of carrying the coffin can be seen as symbolizing the transition of the dead person to the world of the dead. Prior to birth one is carried by a woman but following death the male takes over the role of carrier. Men came into prominence once the body had left the home; they were involved in a visible manner in the final separation and incorporation.

There were differences in the retention of customs and their observance in the midlands. In the material collected in north Roscommon, in the late 1930s, it was apparent that a lot of the old customs were beginning to die out and some were no longer practised. In the same period in south-west Roscommon, on the Galway border, it was recorded that traditional practices were still being observed. In some of the earlier folklore, the collectors were also the narrators and, generally speaking, they were faithful chroniclers of the tradition they recorded.

Most of James Delaney's work focused on the counties adjoining the River Shannon and the customs in these areas were very similar. There was frequent travel along and across the river, especially during the nineteenth and early twentieth centuries, when boats were the mode of transport. This area of east and south Roscommon and the adjoining parts of counties Longford, Westmeath and Offaly were particularly rich in folklore and some of the customs were retained and observed until recently, as is evidenced in the folklore accounts and local knowledge. Evans identified this region as 'a refuge area' and said that these counties of the middle Shannon 'are probably as full of survivals as any in Ireland. This is the land of the loy and the steeveen and the last home of many an ancient custom'.[1] James Delaney shared this view, as can be seen from the concentration of his work on this particular area. He returned to the same narrators again and again, after a lapse of a few months or sometimes years.

In all of the folklore records studied, what stands out is the sense of community and neighbourliness that existed between people in relation to the occasion of death. Death was feared but people accepted it and dealt with it by drawing on their traditional beliefs and customs. Life still had to go on because '*ní chothaíonn an marbh an beo*' [the dead do not sustain the living], but for a time everything was suspended while traditional and religious rituals were observed, so that the significance of the individual's death could be given due recognition. In many of the rituals enacted a sense of respect, affection, and honour was apparent, no matter what people's circumstances were. Traditional practices tempered with religious belief provided people with the means to engage satisfactorily with death. People often did not know why they carried out some of the rituals observed, other than that they were part of a time honoured tradition that marked the transition from the world of the living to that of the dead.

Many of the customs recorded showed a remarkable consistency in tradition but, as is noted in earlier chapters, change was inevitable. Between the 1930s and the 1960s, the social rites associated with death were replaced gradually by religious practices. Society in Ireland had changed remarkably by the middle of the twentieth century and it continued to evolve. The place of death had altered, more people died in hospital and the family and community were no longer directly involved. Tradition is an organic element and it is not surprising that funerary rites changed and will continue to change. In the twenty-first century change is again in evidence in regard to our funerary rites. Due to increased awareness and interest in the psychology of death, people are beginning to realize that the funeral parlour is no substitute for the home. 'Shown the door by society, death is coming back in the window, and it is returning just as quickly as it disappeared'.[2]

Notes

[1] Evans, *Irish Folk Ways*, 18.
[2] Ariès, *The Hour of Our Death*, 560.

Almqvist, Bo, 'The Irish Folklore Commission Achievement and Legacy', *Béaloideas* 45, Dublin (1977), 6-26.

Anon., *Sean-Fhocla Chonnacht*, 1, eag. T. Ó Máille, Baile Átha Cliath, 1948.

Anon., 'Weddings and Wakes', in *The Dublin University Magazine*, 88, Dublin 1876, 292-296.

Aries, Philippe, *Western Attitudes towards Death: From the Middle Ages to the Present*, trans. Patricia M. Ranum, The John Hopkins University Press, Baltimore and London, 1974.

Ariès, Philippe, *The Hour of Our Death*, trans. Helen Weaver, Penguin, London, 1987.

Bardon, Patrick., *The Dead Watchers and Other Folk-Lore Tales of Westmeath*, Mullingar, 1891.

Beirne, Francis, *The Diocese of Elphin: People, Places and Pilgrimage*, The Columba Press, Dublin, 2000.

Carlton, William, *Traits and Stories of the Irish Peasantry, 1*, Garland Publishing, New York, 1979.

Christiansen, Reidar Th., 'The Dead and the Living', *Studia Norvegica* 2, Oslo (1946), 1-96.

Christiansen, Reidar Th., 'Some notes On The Fairies And The Fairy Faith', *Béaloideas* 39, Comhleacht Oideachais na hÉireann, Teo., Baile Átha Cliath (1971), 95-111.

Connolly, S. J., *Priests and People in Pre-Famine Ireland 1780-1895*, Gill and Macmillan, Dublin, 1982.

Coyne, Frank, 'Knockcroghery Clay Pipes', *Roscommon Historical and Archaeological Society 1*, Roscommon (1986), 45-46.

Danagher, Kevin, *In Ireland Long Ago*, Mercier Press, Dublin, 1964.

Douglas, Mary, *Purity and Danger: An analysis of the concepts of pollution and taboo*, Penguin, London, 1979.

Evans, E. Estyn., *Irish Folk Ways*, Routledge and Keegan, London, 1972.

Feilberg, H. F., 'The Corpse-Door: A Danish Survival', *Folk-Lore: A Quarterly Review of Myth, Tradition, Institution and Custom* 18, London (1907), 362-375.

Fennessy, Ignatius, OFM, Franciscan Habit, Fax, July 2003.

Frazer, James G., *The Fear of the Dead in Primitive Religion*, Macmillan and Co., London, 1933.

Gorer, Geoffrey, *Death, Grief and Mourning in Contemporary Britain*, The Cresset Press, London, 1987.

Gailey, Alan, 'A wicker coffin from Ballysheil graveyard, Annaclone, County Down', *Ulster Folklife* 17 (1971), 89-90.

Harbison, Peter, *Pilgrimage in Ireland: The Monuments and the People*, Barrie and Jenkins, London, 1991.

Healy, Paul, *God save all here: memories of life in the twentieth century*, Roscommon, 1999.

Heanue, Mary, 'Matters of Life and Death', in *That was then, This is now*, Central Statistics Office, Dublin 2000, 29-44.

Huntington, Richard, and Metcalf, Peter, *Celebrations of Death The Anthropology of Mortuary Ritual*, Press Syndicate of the University of Cambridge, New York, 1981.

Kligman, Gail, *The Wedding of the Dead: Ritual, Poetics, and Popular Culture in Transylvania*, University of California Press, Berkeley, 1988.

Kselman, Thomas A., *Death and the Afterlife in Modern France*, Princeton University Press, New Jersey, 1993.

Kubler-Ross, Elizabeth, *On Death and Dying*, Touchstone, Simon and Schuster, New York, 1997.

Lamont Brown, R., *A Book of Superstitions*, David & Charles, Newtown Abbot, 1970.

Lucas, A. T., 'Sacred Trees in Ireland', *J.C.H.A.S.* (1963), 16-54.

Lysaght, Patricia, *The Banshee: The Irish Supernatural Death-Messenger*, Glendale Press, Dublin, 1986.

Lysaght, Patricia, 'An Bhean Sí sa Bhéaloideas', in *Gneithe Den Chaointeoireacht*, eag. B. Ó Madagáin, Baile Átha Cliath 1978, 53-66.

Lysaght, Patricia, 'Caoineadh os Cionn Coirp: The Lament for the Dead in Ireland', *Folklore* 108 (1997), 65-82.

Lysaght, Patricia, 'A Chóiste Gan Cheann Dén tAm San Oíche É', *Sinsear, The Folklore Journal* 2, Dublin (1980), 43-59.

Mac Néill, Máire, *The Festival of Lughnasa*, Comhairle Bhéaloideas Éireann, University College Dublin, 1982.

Mág Uidhir, Séamus, 'Pisreóga a Bhaineas leis an mBás', *Béaloideas* 3 (1931), 67-68.

Mannion Joseph, *Saint Kerrill, founder and Patron Saint of Cloonkeenkerrill*, Commemorative Booklet, 2006.

Mannion Joseph, *The life, legends and legacy of Saint Kerrill; a fifth century East Galway evangelist*, Temple Printing Co. Ltd. Athlone, 2004, 99.

Marwick, Ernest W., *The folklore of Orkney and Shetland*, London, B.T. Batsford Ltd., 1975.

Morris, Henry, 'Further Notes on Wake Games', *Bealoideas* 10 (1940), 285-287.

Morris, Henry, 'Irish Wake Games', *Béaloideas* 8, Dublin (1938), 123-141.

Muir, E., *Ritual in Early Modern Europe*, Cambridge University Press, Cambridge, 1997.

Ní Brádaigh, Cáit, 'Folklore from Co. Longford', *Béaloideas* 6, The Educational Company, Dublin (1936), 257-269.

Nic Néill, Máire, 'Wayside Death Cairns in Ireland', *Béaloideas* 16, Educational Company of Ireland (1946), 49-63.

Ó Catháin, Séamus, 'Caointeoireacht an Chine Dhaonna', in *Gnéithe Den Chaointeoireacht*, eag. B. Ó Madagáin, Baile Átha Cliath 1978, 9-19.

Ó Cinnéide, Seán, 'Foclóireacht "Faoi Chlár" agus "Tórramh"', *Feasta* (1980), 19.

Ó Crualaoich, Gearóid, 'The Production and Consumption of Sacred Substances in Irish Funerary Tradition', *Etiainen 2*, Finnish Society for Celtic Studies, Turku (1993), 39-51.

O' Dowd, Peadar, 'Leachta Cuimhne or Funerary Cairns of Wormhole, Moycullen, Co. Galway', *J.G.A.H.S.* (1998), 201-209.

Ó hAilín, Tomás, "Caointe agus Caointeoirí", *Feasta* (1971), 5-9.

Ó Héalaí, Pádraig, 'Gnéithe de Bhéaloideas na Bó: Beannaitheacht agus Piseoga', in *An Bhó*, eag. P. Ó Fiannachta, Dún Chaoin 1992, 61-102.

Ó Madagáin, Breandán, 'Functions of Irish Song in the Nineteenth Century', *Béaloideas* (1985), 130-216.

Ó Muirgheasa, Énrí, 'A Co. Sligo Tradition', *Béaloideas* 2 (1929), 138-139.

Ó Raghallaigh, Colmán, Cluichí Tórraimh in Éirinn: Fianaise An Bhéaloidis, *Tráchtas M.A.* Coláiste na hOllscoile, Gaillimh, 1986.

O Súilleabháin, Seán, *Irish Wake Amusements*, Mercier Press, Cork, 1997.

Ó Súilleabháin, Seán, *A Handbook of Irish Folklore*, Singing Tree Press, Detroit, 1970.

Parker Pearson, Mike, *The Archaeology of Death and Burial*, Sutton Publishing, Gloucestershire, 1999.

Partridge, Angela, *Caoineadh na dTrí Muire*, An Clóchomhar Tta, Baile Átha Cliath, 1983.

Piers, Henry, 'A Chorographical Description of the County of Westmeath', in *Collectanea de Rebus Hibernicis*, 1, Luke White, Dublin 1682, 1-126.

Puckle, Bertram S., *Funeral Customs: Their Origin and Development*, T. Werner Laurie Ltd., London, 1926.

Quinn, Joseph, 'Habit, Religious', in *The Modern Catholic Encyclopedia*, Gill & Macmillan, Dublin 1994, 367.

Rees, Alwyn, and Rees, Brinley, *Celtic Heritage Ancient Tradition in Ireland and Wales*, Thames and Hudson, London, 1961.

Rice, Harry, *Thanks for the Memory*, Colourbooks, Athlone, 1975.

Richardson, Ruth, 'Death's Door: Thresholds and Boundaries in British Funeral Customs', in *Boundaries and Thresholds*, The Thimble Press, Woodchester 1993, 91-102.

Sharper Knowlson, T., *The Origins of Popular Superstitions and Customs*, T. Werner Laurie Ltd., London, 1934.

Shaw Mason, William, *A Statistical Account or Parochial Survey of Ireland*, 2, Dublin, 1814.

Stokes, Margaret, 'Funeral Custom in the Baronies of Bargy and Forth, County Wexford', *J.R.S.A.I.* 4, Dublin (1894), 380-385.

Tohall, Patrick, 'The Diamond Fight of 1795 and the resultant Expulsions', *Seanchas Ardmhacha* 3 (1958).

Tyers, Pádraig, *Malairt Beatha*, Inné Teo., Dún Chaoin, 1992.

van Gennep, Arnold, *The Rites of Passage*, Routledge and Kegan Paul, London, 1977.

Weld, Isaac, *Statistical Survey of the County of Roscommon*, Dublin, 1832.

Wilde, Lady, *Ancient Cures, Charms and Visages of Ireland*, Ward & Downey, London, 1890.

Wilde, William R., *Irish Popular Superstitions*, Irish University Press, Shannon, 1972.

Wilson, Stephen, *The Magical Universe Everyday Ritual and Magic in Pre-Modern Europe*, Hambledon and London, London, 2000.

Witoszek, Nina, and Sheeran, Patrick, *Talking to the Dead: A Study of Irish Funerary Traditions*, Rodopi, Amsterdam, 1998.

Wood-Martin, William G., *Traces of the Elder Faiths of Ireland: A Folklore Sketch*, 1, Kennikat Press, New York, 1902.

IFC: James Hardiman Library, NUI Galway
IFC 79
IFC 194, IFC 195
IFC 549, IFC 552, IFC 571
IFC 653
IFC 714, IFC 782
IFC 1205, IFC 1270
IFC 1399
IFC 1457, IFC 1458, IFC 1487, IFC 1498
IFC 1506, IFC 1507, IFC 1526, IFC 1536, IFC 1550, IFC 1551, IFC 1552, IFC 1573, IFC 1574, IFC 1575
IFC 1610, IFC 1639, IFC 1640, IFC 1641, IFC 1676, IFC 1677
IFC 1736, IFC 1771, IFC 1781, IFC 1782, IFC 1783, IFC 1796
IFC 1834, IFC 1839, IFC 1889

Reader's Notes

Reader's Notes